THE MEDIEVAL CITY STATE

SPECULUM HISTORIALE

GENERAL EDITOR: DENIS SINOR

LATINS IN THE LEVANT
(1204-1566) by W. Miller

BENEDICTINE MONACHISM
by Dom Cuthbert Butler, with a
Foreword by Dom David Knowles

ILLUSTRATIONS OF THE
HISTORY OF MEDIEVAL
THOUGHT AND LEARNING
by R. L. Poole, Second Edition,
revised

THE GOTHIC HISTORY OF
JORDANES
in English Version with an
Introduction and Commentary
by C. C. Mierow

ARTHUR OF BRITAIN
by E. K. Chambers, with a
supplementary bibliography

ANGLO-SAXON INFLUENCE
ON WESTERN CHRISTEN-
DOM (600-800) by S. J. Crawford

THE MEDIEVAL CITY STATE
by M. V. Clarke

THE MEDIEVAL CITY STATE

AN ESSAY ON TYRANNY AND FEDERATION IN THE LATER MIDDLE AGES

BY

M. V. CLARKE, M.A.

FELLOW AND HISTORY TUTOR, SOMERVILLE COLLEGE, OXFORD

CAMBRIDGE: SPECULUM HISTORIALE
NEW YORK: BARNES & NOBLE, INC.

Originally published in 1926 by
Methuen &.Co, Ltd

Reprinted, by permission, without
alteration in 1966 for
SPECULUM HISTORIALE
42 Lyndewode Road, Cambridge

Printed in Great Britain by
Lowe & Brydone (Printers) Ltd,
London

PREFACE

MY thanks are due to Professor F. M. Powicke, Manchester University, and to Mr. E. L. Woodward, All Souls College, Oxford, for their kindness in reading the proofs of this book and for certain valuable corrections of details. Miss M. McKisack, Somerville College, was kind enough to compile the index. In the Bibliography I have attempted to show the extent of my obligation to the published work of other scholars.

M. V. C.

April 1926.

CONTENTS

CHAP.

PREFACE . . . . PAGE
V

I INTRODUCTION I

PART I

PROBLEMS OF INTERNAL GOVERNMENT

II URBAN ECONOMY:

1. Town Origins 9
2. The Rise of Commerce 18
3. The Rise of Industry 26
4. Conclusion 34

III THE PATRICIATE:

1. The Struggle for Emancipation . . 40
2. The Formation of the Patrician Oligarchy 50
3. The Patriciate in Italy 59

IV THE STRUGGLE AGAINST THE PATRICIATE:

1. Introductory 68
2. Florence and Siena 72
3. Germany 86

V THE RISE OF TYRANNY IN ITALY:

1. Introductory 99
2. The Rise of the *Signoria* in Italy . . 105
3. The Development of the Practice and Theory
   of Tyranny 126

vii

PART II

THE STRUGGLE FOR SURVIVAL

CHAP.   PAGE

VI FEDERATION AND DEFENCE IN ITALY:

      1. Introductory 147
      2. Italian Federal Experiments . . . 151
      3. Italian Military and Territorial Policy . 156

VII FEDERATION AND DEFENCE IN GERMANY:

      1. Imperial Policy 167
      2. Leagues of Defence in southern and western
         Germany 172
      3. The Hanseatic League 178

VIII THE SWISS CONFEDERATION OF CITIES AND CANTONS:
      1. Historical Survey 193
      2. The Federal Structure 200

    BIBLIOGRAPHY 209

    INDEX 213

THE MEDIEVAL CITY STATE

CHAPTER I

INTRODUCTION

CENTRAL government and local government form the main natural divisions of the sphere of government. They are normally hostile to each other and their reconciliation is perhaps the most difficult of all constitutional problems. By the middle of the thirteenth century that hostility had already begun to be defined. Castile and Aragon, the Scandinavian countries, France and England were national monarchies, in which government was carried on from the centre to the detriment of feudal and local rights. The general political tendency in these countries was towards absolutism. In Italy, Germany and the Netherlands, where in spite of growing national feeling there was no progress of a constructive kind towards the national state, a strong central government was lacking. Anarchy was averted only by the vigour of local institutions, characterised by a general political tendency towards democracy.

The contrast between these two groups of countries can be seen most clearly in the failure of Italy, Germany and the Netherlands to develop centralised institutions, especially on the judicial side. Both Italy and the Netherlands lacked even the outward forms of central government. The Papacy, as a secular power, was not even *primus inter pares.* In Germany the revival of the Empire gave a delusive appearance of unity, but after the fall of the Hohenstaufen imperial policy lost coherence and became more and more territorial. Neither imperial nor papal influence was exerted consistently or with uniformity. It is true that Popes and Emperors from time to time attempted to solve those structural problems which confront every organised unit of political society, but they invariably failed to secure that national acquiescence which is the necessary condition of strong monarchy. The real political interest centres round the less conspicuous solutions produced by urban societies, by the Teutonic Order, and by the free cantons of the Alps.

In spite of remarkable superficial differences, the problem of government confronting all human groups at an early stage is essentially the same. A degree of order is essential to social well-being ; a degree of progress is, less universally, admitted to be desirable : the best government is that which makes progress possible without sacrificing order. Every social unit, however small, was moved by two psychological forces ; a sense of individual right and a sense of the value of leadership. The sense of individual right, developed first within the family, showed itself most clearly in the transformation of habit into custom and of custom into law. The sense of the value of leadership —which is what Carlyle meant by Hero Worship—showed itself first in Heroic Kingship and later in National Monarchy. Human societies illustrate the continued action of these two forces. Sometimes they balance each other, sometimes one is in excess. When they balance, harmony follows the adjustment of the rights of individuals and the collective interest ; when one is in excess, society oscillates between despotism and anarchy.

The larger the social group, the stronger the tendency to sacrifice custom to leadership, to prefer monarchy to primitive democracy. In the smaller social groups individual rights were much more tenacious, especially if conditions of life did not provoke any demand for strong leadership. In such societies democracy can be studied in its natural and simplest forms, as, for example, in the forest cantons of the Alps. The interest of early Swiss history lies mainly in the fact that it provides us with an example of the stuff out of which political life has developed ; it reveals a series of social groups, which, by reason of special circumstances, did not feel the need of leadership sufficiently to cause them to abandon full individual rights, and presents the natural starting point for any enquiry into the medieval theory and practice of government. In the thirteenth century the rural cantons of the Alps were pure democracies, governing themselves by meetings of the people, in which every householder was the equal of every other. The problems of government with which they had to deal were mainly economic ; they related to the administration of the forests and the distribution of pasture lands, especially the summer pastures of the high Alps. The cantons were economically self-sufficing ; the population lived on the produce of its fields, woods and pastures and was secluded from outside interference by mountains and snow fields. Unity of economic interests prepared the way for political unity of a democratic kind and at the same time fostered a strong sense of individual liberties and rights.

Rural democracy in Switzerland was the direct product of social and economic conditions. As there was no social complexity or economic inequality, all the problems of government were simple and could be solved by simple people. But primitive democracy becomes impossible as soon as existence is complicated by a number of conflicting interests, though, unless the more complex stage is reached, society remains static. Hence political interest must shift from the Alpine cantons to the towns, where a vigorous effort was made to retain or achieve a communal form of government without sacrificing initiative. The medieval town was a social unit, large and crowded enough to be complicated, and small enough to fix the attention of its inhabitants on the business of government. Where the weakness or absence of a central authority permitted free urban development, town history supplies us with political history of a microcosmic kind.

In studying the political history of the towns of Italy and Germany, the predominating interest is structural and other developments, often very important in themselves, must be treated as by-products. On the political side, the subject falls into two divisions, both determined by the unconscious purpose of the town itself. One is concerned with internal development, the other with external relations ; the internal movement of the towns was towards democracy, the external, towards political sovereignty. These two movements were not reciprocal, except in the early stages of town development. In fact, they were often mutually antagonistic, as determination to achieve or maintain full political sovereignty often brought about the sacrifice of democratic government. Thus Venice achieved content under a rigid oligarchy, and many other Italian cities submitted to tyranny. Yet the democratic tendency was always present, even if deeply submerged, and it almost invariably found expression, if other forms of government were discredited. Florence, for example, at the time of the French invasion of 1494, expelled the Medici and re-established a republic.

The historic basis of urban life was originally democratic, though social and economic inequality was certainly present from the beginning. The whole community informally delegated authority to magistrates, who were usually men of wealth and business experience. The object of the community was to provide itself with institutions which would make both progress and order possible. Until the community found at least a temporary solution for the problem of providing itself with the apparatus of government there was no time or energy for internal conflict. Once the towns had secured their autonomy they became conscious of the tendency which distinguished them from other political groups, a tendency which showed itself in a denial of the right of any individual, section or caste in their communities to exercise supreme power. In the national monarchies of Western Europe subjects were willing to acknowledge the executive authority of the king, though they might quarrel over the way in which it was exercised. In the cities of Italy and the Empire it was admitted as a political axiom that all power was ultimately vested in the whole body of citizens. Constitutional development followed the line of increasing the positive control of the people over their government and decreasing the natural inequality of social classes. This democratic tendency, thwarted and blocked by a variety of political and economic obstacles, was the driving force behind the internal struggles of the free cities of the Middle Ages. In north Italy it showed itself strongest in the eleventh and twelfth centuries ; in central Italy, Germany and the Netherlands it developed mainly between 1200 and 1500.

· Urban society seemed to fall naturally into three divisions, determined mainly by economic conditions and aided by the medieval habit of forming corporations, which broke up the community into separate sectional bodies. These three classes were the Patriciate or small group of capitalists, the craft guilds or middle class, representing small scale industries and retail trade, and the proletariate of wage-earners, employed by the Patriciate or by the craft guilds. Internal struggles in the town were, therefore, necessarily three-cornered. At first the wage-earners supported the craft guilds against the Patriciate ; later the craft guilds became alarmed at the demands of the wage-earners and formed coalitions with the Patriciate against them. In the twelfth and thirteenth centuries municipal government was almost entirely in the hands of the Patricians. The emancipation of the cities from outside control, the formation of civic institutions and the growth of a financial and commercial policy were the work of the Patriciate. About the middle of the thirteenth century the craft guilds began to challenge the political monopoly of the Patriciate and to demand a share in the government. The struggle was long drawn out and the results varied from place to place. Sometimes the craft guilds were admitted to a share in municipal government without any serious conflict, as in Dortmund in Westphalia. Sometimes the Patriciate was strong enough to resist all attempts to disturb it, as in Venice and Nuremburg. Sometimes the citizens wearied of the struggle and submitted themselves to the tyranny of an individual or a family as, for example, in Florence to the Medici or in the Flemish towns to Van Artevelde. Sporadic risings of the wage earners were general in the fourteenth and early fifteenth centuries, but they invariably failed to gain political power for more than a very short interval. The general result of the struggle was that the democratic tendency was either modified or obliterated by a majority recognition of the value of leadership, usually expressing itself in oligarchy or tyranny.

The movement towards political sovereignty was stronger and more enduring than the movement towards democracy. It was at first a struggle for emancipation, later a struggle for survival. The enemies of the town were local territorial princes, other powerful urban communities, and the Pope and the Emperor as lords paramount. The need for organised resistance to these enemies helped to determine the internal political development of the town. Liberty often meant little else than freedom from external control and to achieve the status of a sovereign state became the dominating political idea of all great cities. From the end of the thirteenth century even maintenance of independence became difficult, as the policy of territorial consolidation was pushed further and further by kings and princes. Civic liberties were threatened by the territorial ambitions of the Emperors, the German princes, the house of Burgundy, the Italian tyrants, and the Pope. The problem of survival became the dominating problem of the autonomous city.

The fundamental weaknesses of the city were its sterility in food production, its small population and the preoccupations of its citizens. Left to itself it could neither support nor defend its inhabitants. Without the continuous importation of food stuffs, its population was doomed to starvation ; without the help of the man power of the country, it was unable to withstand its enemies. Economic and military necessities made the adoption of a territorial policy essential to survival. The problem was handled differently north and south of the Alps. In Italy the cities absorbed the rural areas by conquest and held them by superior force. For the work of conquest and defence they depended more and more on hired mercenaries, led by adventurers whose ambitions were a constant menace. No attempt was made to secure the co-operation of the conquered areas in the government of the city state ; their population was deprived of all political rights and was usually ready to seize any opportunity to rebel or to combine with invading armies. North of the Alps the cities tried to strengthen their position by forming leagues or federations of a permanent kind. The Rhine League, the Suabian League and the Hanseatic League were organisations of cities undertaken for purposes of defence and protection of commerce. Mutual jealousies and failure to absorb the hinterland of the cities prevented these Leagues from achieving or maintaining their independence.

The problem of the co-operation of town and country, without the sacrifice of the independence of either, was solved only in Switzerland. There, by a voluntary federation of cities and free cantons, state sovereignty was established on a permanent basis. The common danger of Habsburg aggression made the cantons willing to supply the cities with food and soldiers ; the cities in return provided the cantons with markets and put at their disposal a wider knowledge of commercial conditions and of European politics.   Thus in the study of the medieval city state the interest must ultimately centre in Switzerland, as in the study of Parliamentary history the interest centres in England.   In Federation lay the only hope of preserving the civic unit.   The Italians rejected the federal idea and relied on physical force ; the Germans and Netherlanders adopted it, but used it in an eclectic and undemocratic form.   The Swiss admitted the democratic principle as the basis of their federal policy and combined town and country in an organic whole.   By this means they were able to resist the rise of absolutism and the land hunger of the great powers, which destroyed the liberties of the cities of Italy, Germany and the Netherlands.

PART I

PROBLEMS OF INTERNAL GOVERN-MENT

CHAPTER II

URBAN ECONOMY [1]

TOWN ORIGINS. THE RISE OF COMMERCE. THE RISE OF INDUSTRY. CONCLUSION.

I. TOWN ORIGINS

THE beginning of urban life does not in itself require an elaborate explanation, as it was inevitable in all countries passing out of the primitive pastoral stage. Towns grew up naturally where there were fortifications, churches or markets and acquired certain rights of self-protection in the process. We can first speak of a town when a particular place forms a legal and administrative area for itself alone, when it is enclosed by walls, and when it has market rights and a special peace and obtains a special preference over the open country with regard to public burdens. Once an area was protected by walls it had the special peace of a fortified place ; it became the natural residence of local potentates, a centre of jurisdiction and a market. Normally, new urban units easily found a

[1] In this chapter I have not attempted to do more than indicate economic factors important for my general thesis.

place in the territorial organisation of the country and remained under the control of the Monarch or Prince responsible for government. The history of towns in England and, to a less extent, in France, Castille and Aragon illustrates a natural economic development of secondary political importance. In Italy, Germany and the Netherlands, where the central power was weak, the towns were able to achieve independence and, sometimes, to maintain and develop it so that it became, not local government, but collective sovereignty.

It is possible to divide towns according to their origin into three main groups : (1) Towns on Roman sites ; (2) Towns which were the natural product of medieval social conditions ; (3) Artificial town creations. A brief examination of this classification is necessary, as the later history of a town was to a certain extent determined by conditions of origin.

Towns on Roman sites cannot, even in Italy, establish any claim to continuity of political life from the classical period. The Roman tradition of municipal government was broken. The Romans bequeathed nothing to the medieval urban community except their fortifications and the habit of living in towns. Towns on Roman sites arose all over Italy, and in the valleys of the Rhine and the Danube. They were unknown in central and north-eastern Germany and, owing to Norse invasions, in the Netherlands. Italian historians often regard the rise of the commune as the triumph of Roman over Teutonic civilisation. Roman imperial society was for a long time organised on a municipal basis and had consisted of an aggregate of cities exercising powers of self-government under the control of the Capital. Teutonic society, on the other hand, was organised on a more primitive territorial basis ; its unit of government was, not the city, but the *gau, comitatus, county* or *contado*, ruled over by the *comes* or his deputy.

When the Lombards conquered Italy in the sixth century
they divided it into ninety-six duchies under *duces* ; below
the *duces* were *comites* ruling over counties and, sometimes,
below them were *sculdascii* or bailiffs. The king was
nominal overlord, but actually each grade struggled to
emancipate itself from the control of superior authority.
In the eighth century the Franks overthrew the whole
structure, except in the south ; the territory was redis-
tributed but the *contado* was retained as the unit of organisation. Border provinces known as *Marches* and governed
by a *margrave* or *marquis*, were set up and a barbarian
nobility of margraves and counts became the ruling class in
Italy. They were indifferent to the population gathered in
the Roman sites and lived almost entirely in the country.
Probably from the first they were partially dependent on
the trade of the conquered population and were compelled
to grant privileges and immunities in return for commodities. Their energy was almost entirely occupied by
the long struggle with the Emperors in the ninth and tenth
centuries. The spiritual princes, the bishops, seized the
opportunity to establish themselves behind fortifications
and secured from the Emperors grants of temporal power
over the towns. A very similar process went on, though
more slowly, in south and west Germany. Part of the wall
circuits of the Roman towns survived and were gradually
filled by settlers. The Germans themselves were ignorant
of urban life and the Franks gave the Roman sites no
special place in their organisation. They became episcopal
residences and were called *civitates*. Owing to immunities
obtained by the bishops, the episcopal centres were
withdrawn from the ordinary jurisdiction of the county
and became separate judicial areas. The survival of
the old Roman squares and the carefully chosen geographical position of the site helped to revive gradually
markets and commercial intercourse. Such a revival
took place at Bâle, Zurich, Constance, Regensburg,

Strassburg, and Cologne and also in the Upper Danube basin.[1]

Towns which were the product of medieval social conditions were rare in Italy where the best town sites had nearly always been occupied by the Romans. An important exception is Venice, founded in the lagoons of the north-west Adriatic by refugees fleeing from the barbarian invaders. The islets, *lidi* or banks of sand and sediment formed by the Alpine rivers Brenta and Adige were sparsely inhabited until, from the fifth century (A.D.) onwards, fugitives from the cities of Lombardy and central Italy began to settle there. We know of the existence of twelve island townships at an early date ; by the end of the seventh century the settlers on the island of the Rialto (Venice) had elected their first duke or doge and by the middle of the ninth century they were exercising hegemony over the other islands. North of the Alps towns began to develop in well-populated districts favourably suited for commerce. In the Netherlands early urban development was due primarily to excellence of geographical situation. When the Norse invasions came to an end the lower basins of the Rhine, the Meuse and the Scheldt became the meeting place of two streams of traffic, one coming from the Baltic and North Sea and the other from the Mediterranean by way of the Rhine and the Rhone. The *portus*, market or place through which commerce regularly passed, appeared on these commercial routes. In Germany opportunities for urban development were not so great and the rise of new towns was slower, less vigorous and less independent. In the south and west older towns on Roman sites were the natural centres of industry and commerce

[1] The Roman frontier in Germany at the beginning of the second century A.D. followed the Rhine up river to Bonn (*Bonna*), crossed to a point on the Danube near Ratisbon (*Reginum*) in modern Bavaria and then followed the Danube south-east to its junction with the Theiss near Belgrade. The frontier between Bonn and Ratisbon was protected along the greater part of the way by a wall.

and specially favourable circumstances were necessary before new towns could compete with them. Lucerne, for example, was at first of purely local importance as a distributing centre for the products of the adjacent Alpine valleys, but when the S. Gotthard route to Italy was opened, (*c.* 1236), it became one of the most important commercial stations between Lombardy and the Upper Rhine. In central and northern Germany towns grew up round the fortifications of a secular prince, the residence of a bishop or the buildings of an abbey. At first these places were simply gatherings round a seignorial *Hof*, *Curtis* or Court, or a *Dorf* or village ; when they also became markets and centres of industry they can be called towns. For example, Goslar in the Hartz mountains was first used as a hunting lodge by the Franconian Emperors. The discovery of precious metals in the adjacent mountain encouraged settlers to come and in the middle of the eleventh century Henry III declared it to be a *Pfalz stadt*, (Palatinate town), and caused a palace and cathedral to be built. Magdeburg, Lüneburg and Bremen had a similar origin. Dortmund represents another type of natural urban development ; it was formed out of a union of several rural communes and owed its importance to its position on the main road between the Rhine and the Weser.[1] Both in Germany and the Netherlands towns which were the product of social and economic conditions were directly dependent on the protection and favour either of the Emperor or, much more often, of a local prince.

Artificial town creations were unknown in the Netherlands, where the commercial and industrial vigour of a relatively dense population made them unnecessary ; for similar reasons they were rare in Italy. In Germany the foundation of towns was the normal means adopted by both Emperors and princes to defend and develop their territories. The town was legally created by means of a

[1] Cf. Soest and Munster.

2

written charter. Sometimes peasant communities were
granted urban rights, but more often a special area was
set aside as a town site, settlers were invited and a ready-
made constitution was granted after the model of those
which older towns had already developed for themselves.
Imperial towns were most often founded by grants of
market rights and at first the Emperor alone could
establish a market. When in the twelfth century princes
began to give away market privileges and found towns for
themselves they were usurping imperial prerogatives.
The practice of town foundation spread from the south-west
to the east and north. The great house of Zähringen, which
dominated the Western Alps and Upper Burgundy in
the twelfth century, probably began the policy of the foundation of towns by princes. The free customs granted,
(1120), by Conrad of Zähringen to Freiburg in Breisgau were
not only exemplars for many places in the Upper Rhineland,
but probably helped to bring about Henry the Lion's more
famous foundations of Munich, Brunswick and Lübeck,
(1158). The towns from which the constitution of new
foundations were borrowed maintained a curious legal
connection with daughter towns. When municipal
customary law was obscure or defective the mother town
acted as a superior court and by means of this dependent
relationship numerous families of town constitutions were
formed. The most famous *Mutterrechte* were those of
Lübeck and Magdeburg. The customary law of Lübeck
was derived from Soest and was handed on to a number
of daughter cities on the Baltic coast.[1] The constitution
of Magdeburg was adopted by many inland towns in the
north-east, so that Magdeburg *Stadtrecht* became almost as
important as the *Sachenspiegel*, (the thirteenth century law
book or custumal of Saxony,) in the legal system of the east.[2]

[1] E.g. Wismar, Rostock, Greifswald and Kolberg.
[2] The *Schöffen* of Magdeburg gave the following decisions for the
town of Kulm in 1338.
1. " May a *Ratman* be deposed ? . . . You have asked us in

The Zähringen family and Henry the Lion were the only successful founders of towns in the south;[1] other foundations by secular princes were of small importance.

Conditions were entirely different in the north where there were no Roman sites and where the work of colonization at the expense of Scandinavians and Slavs was carried on without much interference from the Emperors or the Church. All along the Baltic coast and in the river basins of the Elbe, the Oder and the Vistula, towns were founded where organised urban life had hitherto been unknown. Places first used by the Germans as military stations were granted municipal privileges and gradually became centres of industry and commercial distribution. The most important of these artificial town creations of the north was Lübeck. Count Adolf II of Holstein was the first to recognise the importance of a small river island on the River Trave at the point where it was still navigable for deep water ships. Its position in the south-west corner of the Baltic Coast made it a natural haven for all foreign shipping. Its land communications were excellent, as it was in easy reach of the Elbe basin.[2] Count Adolf invited settlers to

your letter whether the burggrave may depose some of the *Rat-männer* and appoint others in their place. We answer that . . . The burggrave has no right to depose *Ratmänner* and put others in their place.

9. Concerning Taxes. You further asked us, if the citizens have property outside the territory of the city . . . are they bound to pay the tax which may be assessed on such property just as they pay it on their ordinary property. We answer that, according to the law and practice of our city, every man must pay taxes on his property outside as well as inside the city, no matter where it is " (*Vide* Altmann u. Bernheim : Urkunden No. 210 pp. 442–444).

Cf. the *Mutterrechte* of Dortmund, Cleve, Aachen and Vienna.

[1] The best examples of their work were Munich and Berne. Munich was raised from obscurity by the grant of a mint and a salt market in 1158. Berne was founded in 1191 by Count Berthold V. of Zähringen to protect communications between Berthoud and Friburg.

[2] When the Steckenitz canal was cut between Lübeck and Hamburg (1390–8) water communications with the North Sea became independent of the control of the Baltic Straits.

his new town from Westphalia, Flanders and Frisia. He allotted sites for houses and land for cultivation and established a bailiff or *Vogt* who co-operated with the settlers in the work of governing the community. In 1158 Henry the Lion took over the town from Count Adolf, and did all he could to develop its commerce. Helmold, a contemporary chronicler, states that he offered free trading to all the lands of the north and east, Norway, Sweden, Denmark and Russia, established a mint and tolls, and gave the townspeople special privileges, and a constitution borrowed from the town of Soest.

In 1181 Frederick Barbarossa overthrew Henry the Lion and seized Lübeck for himself. Seven years later, (1188), in response to an appeal for protection, he gave it a charter of liberties. Certain rights of self-government were admitted and confirmed ; the personal freedom of denizens was recognised and their merchants were exempt from all tolls throughout the Duchy of Saxony. The protection of the Emperor, though mainly of a negative kind, enabled Lübeck to survive the fall of Henry the Lion and the period of Danish predominance in the Baltic, (c. 1202–41). In 1226 Frederick II definitely recognised it as an imperial city and bestowed upon it further privileges. By the middle of the fourteenth century it was the wealthiest city in the north. Lübeck ships traded with the whole Baltic region and brought back rich cargoes of raw material, used either in home industries or for export to the Netherlands and England. According to a recent estimate, 800 ships or a total of 20,000 tons were engaged in the carrying trade of Lübeck in the fifteenth century. Its prosperity was the chief factor in the commercial and industrial development of the whole of the North German plain. If Lübeck were the greatest single town creation, the greatest series of such creations was that which followed the conquest of Prussia and the Baltic provinces in the north-east by the Teutonic Knights. In 1231–2 they conquered and occupied the upper Vistula basin and founded the towns of Thorn and Kulm, to which they gave the constitution and laws of Magdeburg. Within the next decade, (1233–41) the Lower Vistula basin was conquered and Marienwerder and Elbing were founded with similar privileges. Elbing was populated by settlers from Lübeck, attracted by its favourable situation near the land-locked Frisches Haff, and by the year 1250 its government was organised on the Lübeck model. After the Union of the Teutonic Knights with the Knights of the Sword, who had conquered Livonia, the towns of Braunsberg and Pernau were founded. Königsberg on the Baltic coast about seventy miles north of Elbing, was founded by King Ottocar of Bohemia in 1255. In the interior of both East and West Prussia various other towns were founded with constitutions based on that of Kulm, which had in turn been borrowed from Magdeburg in 1232. The Teutonic Order was at first so generous in granting charters of liberties that the Prussian towns became almost independent political units. They enjoyed full rights of self-government within their walls and at the same time benefited by the general commercial policy of the Order. At least eighty-five towns were founded, many of which became extremely wealthy. Later, as members of the Hanseatic League, they became clearing houses for the products of Russia and Poland and employed commercial agents in Novgorod and Warsaw in the East and in London and Bergen on the West.

Lübeck and the towns of Prussia are only the most famous examples of a policy followed by the territorial rulers of the north German plain from the middle of the twelfth to the end of the thirteenth century. The result can be seen at a glance if a map of Germany in the reign of Rudolf is examined. German predominance had been asserted and maintained at the expense of the Danes and Slavs all along the southern coast of the Baltic, about 250 German miles in extent. In less than a century and a half sixteen towns of the first class had grown up, whose prosperity was dependent on industry and overseas commerce.[1]   The unity of the south coast of the Baltic and its inclusion within the German Empire could have been achieved in no other way.   Urban development on so large a scale tended to redress the unequal balance between North and South.

2.   THE DEVELOPMENT OF COMMERCE

In the Dark Ages many difficulties hindered the growth of commercial intercourse, not only between Europe and Asia, but between Christian countries not far distant from each other.   Land was the chief form of wealth and land was an unsatisfactory medium of exchange.   The absence of a credit system and the diversity of weights, measures and currencies prevented free exchange other than barter. Feudal or manorial economy was self-sufficient, producing within a narrow circle all the necessities of life : consequently, the demand for imported commodities was small.   A strong prejudice, fostered by the Church, existed against the merchant, who was regarded as a parasite, speculator and usurer.   The first merchants were persons outside the feudal circle of organisation, that is, strangers—often Jews—who could not expect much protection from the government to counterbalance popular hostility.   Their activities were further limited by the incurious and conservative attitude of consumers and by general ignorance of geography.   The greater part of Europe was thinly populated and large areas of waste, marsh and forest rendered communication and transport very difficult.   In such circumstances initiative was bound to come, not from the territorial kingdoms or feudal principalities, but from urban areas, where economic life

[1] Lübeck in Holstein : Wismar and Rostock in Mecklenburg ; Stralsund, Greifswald and Stettin in Pomerania ; Danzig, Elbing, Kulm, Thorn, Braunsberg and Königsburg in Prussia ; Pernau, Riga, Reval and Dorpat in Livonia and Esthonia.

had ceased to be a matter of fixed routine, and had acquired certain artificial characteristics.

The development of grand commerce in Western Europe dates from the First Crusade, at the end of the eleventh century. The Crusades broke down barriers of ignorance between East and West and commerce followed Crusaders and pilgrims into Palestine, Syria, Sicily, and Spain. For the first time since the envelopment of the Mediterranean basin by the Moslems in the seventh century the sea was open for full commercial intercourse between East and West. The Italian cities alone were ready to profit at once by the new intercourse and, through their activities, the Mediterranean basin became the centre of exchange between East and West and North and South. Northern cities gradually began to take their share in the work of distribution and by this means new centres of trade were developed along the old military and pilgrim routes of France and the Empire. The power of commerce soon showed itself in the growth of urban republics, in the appearance of new markets and fairs and in the discovery and protection of trade routes. At the same time local trade and exchange were stimulated by the enterprise and activity of grand commerce.

From the twelfth century onwards the great trade routes of western merchants fall into two divisions : trade routes between Europe and Asia and trade routes between the Mediterranean and transalpine Europe.[1] Venice was the connecting link between the two systems. Her merchants brought oriental wares from the Asiatic routes which had their *termini* in the Black Sea, in the Levant and in Egypt. From Venice goods were transported over the Alps to Northern Europe. The most important route ran from Venice over the Brenner Pass to Innsbruck : from Inns-

[1] Important commercial relations developed between the population of the North African coast and the cities of Italy, Provence and Catalonia.

bruck tributary routes branched out fan-wise to all points
of the compass. An eastern route followed the Inn to
Regensburg and thence down the Danube to Vienna : a
northern route passed through Augsburg and Nuremburg to
Lower Germany : a western route ran by Ulm, Constance
and Bâle to the Upper Rhone valley and the basin of the
Seine. Another main route ran from Venice up the Po
valley to Milan and thence over the Splügen Pass to
Constance : from Constance roads ran east to Augsburg,
west to the Upper Rhone and north along the Rhine
Valley to the Netherlands. A later variant of this route
crossed the S. Gotthard Pass to Bâle. The Splügen and
S. Gotthard Passes were used by all the merchants of Italy,
but the Brenner Pass became almost a Venetian monopoly.
These routes illustrate the dependence of towns in Upper
Germany on Italian trade, a dependence increased by the
fact that the Danube route to the Black Sea was disturbed
by the eruption of the Tartars and was never fully developed
owing to the backward civilisation of the peoples of
Hungary, Moldavia and Bulgaria. The connection
between Venice and Augsburg, Regensburg and Nuremburg was very close. A *Fondaco dei Tedeschi* or German
Chamber of Commerce was established in Venice as early
as 1228. Young German merchants of the South were sent
to study business methods in Venice in the same way as
sons of northern merchants served an apprenticeship in
Bruges, Bergen and London. As a result, the towns of
Upper Germany borrowed much of Italian culture and the
effect can be seen in their art, literature and politics. The
merchant cities of Lower Germany for some time remained
backward in culture. They were in direct contact with
savage or heathen lands ; the commodities they handled
were raw materials and the necessities of life rather than
the luxuries of the Orient : their profits were acquired by
harder work and greater risks : The hostility between them
and the southern merchants in the later Middle Ages was

due as much to difference in culture as to commercial competition. The meeting-point of North and South was in the Netherlands where the routes from Asia and southern Europe, from Novgorod and the Baltic converged.

The development of trade routes was necessarily accompanied by improvements in the means of transport and greater security for merchant caravans. Roads began to be kept in repair, bridges were built and small-draught sailing ships and barges were used as river transport. Safe-conducts for foreign merchants began to be guaranteed in treaties. Magna Carta, for example, provided that " all merchants should have safe and secure exit from England and entry into England, with the right to tarry there and move about as well by land as by water, for purposes of buying and selling. . . ." A post service was established in Italy by the middle of the twelfth century; by means of it a message could be sent from Florence to Naples in five or six days. A similar service was established in Germany about 1237. Transport facilities had improved so much that by the thirteenth century heavy merchandise could be sent from Genoa to Paris in thirty-five days.

Maritime commerce was developed in the Mediterranean chiefly by the cities of Venice, Pisa, Genoa, Marseilles and Barcelona. Venice laid the foundation of her maritime commerce in a treaty with the Byzantine Emperor signed in 1082. Not much more than a century later, (1204), she made use of the deflection of the Fourth Crusade to acquire a colonial empire in the Archipelago, to seize the keys of the Dardanelles and the Bosphorus and to establish commercial relations with the Far East. Genoa established commercial depots in Corsica, Chios, and at Kaffa on the Black Sea and, having crushed her nearest rival, Pisa, entered into a life and death struggle with Venice for the commercial hegemony of the Eastern Mediterranean.

Venice proved the victor and became the commercial capital of southern Europe. At the beginning of the fifteenth century she had a navy of 3,300 ships manned by 36,000 sailors and her imports represented a third of the total imports of Italy with a yearly value of ten million francs. Other Italian cities, especially Genoa and Florence, shared in the profits of a commerce which included trade not only with Asia Minor, but also with North Africa, South-East Russia and the Far East. In northern and western Europe the growth of maritime commerce began in the sea and river ports of the Netherlands about the time when the Norman conquest brought England into closer contact with the continent. Grand commerce in the Baltic can be traced to the foundation of Lübeck and to the colonisation of Prussia in the middle of the thirteenth century. The subsequent union of northern cities in the Hanseatic League helped to secure for the cities of Lower Germany a commercial monopoly in the Baltic Sea.

The directors of all this activity were the great merchants and bankers who specialised in the handling of raw materials and such luxury products as spices, silks, furs and delicate fabrics. Their transactions brought about important financial developments, as they required both capital and credit. In the twelfth century standard coinages were adopted by the more enlightened Italian cities, by the Norman rulers of England and of the two Sicilies and by the Count of Flanders. A system of credit was established with a rate of interest very much lower than that which the Jews, owing to the insecurity of their position, were able to offer. In the thirteenth century the Jewish charge on loans was between forty and fifty per cent., while Christian merchants and bankers in Italy and south Germany were charging something between ten and seventeen per cent. The letter of credit, already in use among the Greeks and the Arabs, was adopted by Italians, Provençals, Catalans and Flemings. The Jews gradually lost their financial predominance and gave place to Italian merchant bankers. Between the middle of the twelfth and the middle of the fourteenth centuries, Lombards, Genoese, Sienese, Lucchese and Florentines were the masters of international commerce and finance. In 1292 there were sixteen Italian business houses in Paris and many others in London, Montpellier, Nîmes, Naples and Barcelona. Through their use of credit, the Italians became bankers as well as merchants, and, as business developed, men began to prefer to invest their money in commerce rather than to hoard it in their houses or deposit it in monasteries. The chief obstacle in the way of progress in banking was the emphatic prohibition of usury by Canon Law, based on the text : " Give to him that asketh, hoping for nothing again." Italian financiers evaded ecclesiastical penalties by a number of casuistical devices. For example, the idea was developed that interest was compensation for delay in the repayment of the original loan. A merchant could with a clear conscience contract to receive interest from persons to whom he lent money, provided that he first lent it gratuitously for a period which might be very short. Technically, interest was not reward for use but compensation for failure to repay. The gratuitous period soon disappeared, or was made so short that it became a mere formality. Justifications of credit and loan transactions were developed along these lines by the great civilian lawyer, Accursius (c. 1220–60), by Alexander of Hales and by S. Thomas Aquinas. Italian bankers made their position secure by taking the Church into dependent partnership and by advancing loans to Popes and prelates in return for pledges of land, precious stones or plate. The banks, formed by a union of a number of merchants of the same family or of the same town, soon began to use their financial power to control markets in their own interests. As their capital increased, they established agents all over Europe and in Syria, Cyprus and North Africa. Their influence became so great that no important transactions could be undertaken without their financial assistance.[1]

The merchants early adopted a form of organisation for the defence and advancement of their interests, known as *Hansa, Arte* or Guild. In the north these organisations were sometimes united by a federal bond in order to enjoy a commercial monopoly and protection of trade routes. The Hansa of Champagne was organised in connection with the great fair of Champagne ; between the twelfth and the thirteenth centuries its numbers increased from seventeen to sixty members, representing merchant guilds in the cities of North France, Normandy, Brabant and Flanders. The Hansa of London was a similar league organised to control North Sea trade. Its capital was Bruges and the most important of its seventeen members were merchant associations in Ghent, Lille and London. The English Company of the Staple, (founded *c.* 1267), and the Hanseatic League were later developments of the same kind of organisation.

In Flanders the guild merchant was organised at an early date on strictly commercial and capitalist lines. Membership was restricted to persons engaged in wholesale trade, that is, the richest and most enterprising of the burghers. Those who were ruined by financial disaster were expelled from the guild and their places were taken by recruits from the lower ranks of society. An entrance fee of one gold mark excluded the poor ; in addition shopkeepers and hand workers were expressly denied admission. Pirenne states that " if an artisan made money and wished to be enrolled he had to abjure his calling and break with his companions." The guild merchant developed along somewhat similar lines in the commercial cities of West-

---

[1] Edward III could not have begun the Hundred Years War if he had not been able to raise loans from the Florentine Bankers in London, cf. a loan of a million francs raised by the Archbishop of Cologne from Italian bankers in the thirteenth century. Later, the Emperor Charles IV borrowed two millions in one year.

phalia and the Lower Rhine, though only smaller towns
appear to have retained it in a fully organised form.[1]
More commonly the richest and most influential citizens
belonged to a guild which was of social as well as economic
importance, like the *Richerzecke* of Cologne or the *Reinolds-
gilde* of Dortmund. In Germany commerce on a large
scale was slow in developing and at first lacked the necessary support of capitalist banking associations.

In Italy the greater wealth of the towns and the importance of banking caused the growth of more complicated
forms of organisation, as it was often found impossible to
include all the capitalists of a city in a single guild. In
Florence, for example, the *popolo grasso* or rich bourgeoisie
was organised in the Seven Greater Guilds (*Arti Maggiori*),
one of which, the *Arte di Calimala*, bore some resemblance
to the Hansa or Guild Merchant of northern cities. It
was a half-commercial, half-financial syndicate of merchants
with a capitalistic and complex organisation, consisting of
a number of business houses or families, each trading in its
own name, but all submissive to common regulations. The
governing body was composed of the masters, patrons or
capitalist heads of houses ; it was almost impossible for
their employees, (*sottoposti*), to improve their position and
receive any share in the direction of affairs. Great energy
and ability was shown in the conduct and extension of
business. Agents were stationed on all the main trade
routes to provide lodgings for merchants and relays of
draught animals for pack trains and to report on the safety
of roads and bridges. The business of the guild became so
extensive that it developed its own commercial code, which
was adopted by neighbouring countries. Its legal records
were written down, not in Latin, but in the Tuscan dialect,
and it was by this means as much as by the works of the
great Florentine writers that the Tuscan dialect became the
Italian language. By the middle of the thirteenth century

[1] E.g. Göttingen and Hoxter.

there were about eighty banking houses in Florence. By them the letter of credit, which made trade without the transport of specie possible, was developed. Loans were advanced on a pledge system, and investments of capital were invited. They helped in the issue of the gold florin of twenty-four carats, (1252), which was accepted as a standard of value throughout Europe and gave a great impetus to the extension of Florentine commerce. Their chief source of strength lay in their refusal to specialise ; unlike the Jews or Cahorsines they were great merchants as well as dealers in money. By combining the activities of traders, bankers and usurers they made their services essential to all the most prosperous countries and princes of Europe.

Thus the Mediterranean, with Florence as its financial and Venice as its commercial capital, became again the centre from which trade routes radiated throughout Europe, North Africa and Asia. Their success was only the highest point of a general development. The search for markets, the exchange of commodities and the protection of lines of communication broke down barriers of ignorance and indifference and restored something of the old unity of civilisation lost with the Roman Empire. As a result, a monetary economy took the place of primitive or natural economy and capital became an important social and political force. Artisans and peasants, the instruments of economic progress, began to demand a share of political and social influence ; at the same time the wealth and prestige of the great merchants or Patricians made it very difficult to take from them the controlling power.

3. THE DEVELOPMENT OF INDUSTRY

Industrial conditions and their influence on the political life of towns are more easily understood if the development of petty or local industy is considered apart from grand or interregional industry.   Petty industry arose out of an attempt to make the urban unit self-sufficing, just as the manorial unit had been.   To satisfy the needs of the urban population, groups of artisans appeared and very soon they began to supply commodities to the surrounding country in return for agricultural produce and raw material. The exchange of manufactured goods for food and raw material—at first conducted on the barter system— became an essential part of town economy and was therefore carefully controlled by the town government.   This control was exercised in the interests of both consumers and artisans ; its object was to secure good quality at a low rate and at the same time to enable the workers to gain a reasonable reward for industry.   In the interests of the consumer inspectors of industry were employed and standards and methods of work were enforced by severe punishments.   Work was compulsory and a strike was a grave crime.   On the other hand, the interests of the artisans were protected by the exclusion of outside competition, by the guarantee of monopoly rights and by the enforcement of maximum hours of work and minimum prices.

Partly from a sense of common interest and partly to facilitate the supervision of the magistrates, the artisans of particular trades organised themselves in corporations, known as brotherhoods, mysteries, fellowships, arts or guilds.   The number of these associations varied from town to town, according to the stage of industrial development that had been reached : usually the shopkeeper or small retailer was included in the artisan class.   In Germany corporations of artisans appeared under a variety of customary names.   In Cologne they were called *Bruderschaften* (brotherhoods), in the Westphalian towns *Gilden*, in Lübeck, Hamburg and Bremen *Amter* (offices) and in Magdeburg and Stendal *Innungen* (Corporations).   They arose through free agreement and were often at least as old as the Guild Merchant. In Cologne, for example, the bedstuff-makers, including the linen weavers, were granted the right to form a *Bruderschaft* in 1189 and a similar right was granted in 1183 to the Tailors and Shoemakers of Magdeburg. These rights were granted by the Archbishops ; later they were conferred by the *Stadtrat* or town council. The right to form a guild carried with it not only the right to choose officials and make and enforce byelaws, but also *Zunftzwang* or industrial monopoly, which protected members from outside competition and compelled all who followed a particular trade in a city to belong to its guild. In Italian cities *Arti* or guilds were very numerous, and were the chief agents in the development of the wealth and culture of the peninsula. Every trade and nearly every craft had some form of corporate organisation to which was entrusted a certain share in the economic life of the city. In Florence the fourteen *Arti Minori* (lesser guilds) were further subdivided into five middle and nine petty guilds, a division which had later political importance. The five middle guilds were the butchers, iron workers, stone masons and carpenters, linen-drapers, and second-hand dealers. They did not differ much in importance or in organisation from the nine petty guilds of wine-merchants, innkeepers, oil, salt and cheesemongers, tanners, armourers, locksmiths, toolmakers, and tinkers, curriers, wood vendors and ovenkeepers and bakers. The petty trades did not require a large outlay of capital and, in consequence, they retained a democratic form of organisation. Their members were all artisans who worked for themselves in their own shops or homes. The guild looked after the common interest and gave assistance to members disabled by illness or financial calamity. Apprentices and journeymen could reasonably expect to become masters as soon as they had saved the small amount of capital necessary for an independent business. Through the energy of these small associations urban production rapidly increased and the development of large scale industry became possible.

The development of grand or interregional industry was closely connected with grand commerce. It tended to localise itself on the great commercial highways, because merchants were thus able to dispose of the surplus of manufactured products. Metal ware, silk and woollen goods were the chief articles in grand commerce and the most important centres of their manufacture were Italy and the Netherlands. In the Netherlands woollens were manufactured especially at Ypres, Ghent, Bruges, Douai and Louvain : in Italy at Milan, Verona, Modena, Bologna and Florence. In Germany a limited amount was manufactured in the cities of the Rhineland and Upper Germany. Linen and cotton were manufactured in Italy and Flanders, but on a much smaller scale. The centres of the silk industry were South Italy, Florence and Venice. Zurich began to manufacture silk in the fourteenth century. Mineral industries were to a large extent localised in the diocese of Liège, especially at Dinant, and in the mountains of the Hartz, Fichtelgebirge and Erzgebirge ; only in Liège was the industry on a large scale.

These large scale industries were organised under the name of guilds and they seldom advanced as far as the concentration of workers in large factories or workshops. The directors of industry had their offices or clearing houses, which served as depots for the reception of manufactured goods and at which only a few clerks and messengers were employed. From the depots the raw material was distributed to be manufactured under the direction of a number of small masters who worked in their own homes or in small workrooms. The capitalist merchant was the sole purchaser of the manufactured article and he had complete control of its sale in foreign markets. By him sums of money were handed over to the small master, who reserved a portion for himself before paying wages to his

3

assistants. Thus the workers were mere agents of production under direct capitalist control and it was impossible that their guilds could be organised on the same democratic basis as petty industries of only local importance. The necessity of direct connection with foreign markets and the purchase of raw material made necessary the direction and control of industry by capitalist merchants. The workers had no part in the guilds which employed them, because they had neither capital nor commercial experience ; they were mere wage-earners and, as the demand for manufactured goods increased, this wage-earning proletariate came to form a large proportion of the population in towns where grand industry had been developed. Unlike the artisans of the petty guilds, their industry was dependent on foreign markets and was therefore subject to periods of trade depression and unemployment. Even in times of plenty the workers were dependent on capitalist directors of industry, who fixed their wages at the lowest subsistence margin and used their political power to forbid combination of employees.

The true centres of grand industry were Liège, Brabant, Flanders and the cities of North Italy and Tuscany. Of these Florence provides us with the best example of the specialisation of large scale industry and its organisation on a capitalistic basis. In 1306, 100,000 lengths of woollen cloth were manufactured in the city at a total value of a million gold florins ; in 1339 the annual value of manufactured woollen goods was estimated at 1,200,000 gold florins. There was obviously a close connection between the development of industry and increase of population, as Florence enlarged her wall circuit for the second time in 1172 and, not much more than a century later (1299), a third circuit was built which enclosed a still larger area. Abundance of labour made it possible to maintain wages at a low rate. The employees of the great wool and silk guilds were kept outside the guild organisations ; they

had no corporate or political rights. Their wages and hours
of work were fixed by their masters. The whole system
can be illustrated by reference to the organisation of
the *Arte della Lana*, the great guild which controlled the
woollen industry of Florence. The wool was procured
mainly in the cold countries of the North, where rough
cloth was manufactured as a domestic industry. Merchants of the *Arte di Calimala* transmitted it to Florence
to be refined, dyed and enriched for purposes of oriental
trade or for re-export to the countries of its origin. The
Florentines soon became discontented with the imported
cloth and about 1212 an industrial guild was formed to
manufacture it in the city. Raw material was brought
from Spain, France, Germany and England, and the
industry progressed so rapidly that by the end of the
thirteenth century the *Arte della Lana* had a larger capital
and a more stable position than even the *Arte di Calimala*.
Close affiliation of the two guilds was essential ; many
wealthy families, including the Medici, were members of
both. The older guild continued to refine and dye foreign
cloth and the *Arte della Lana* worked from raw material,
often supplied to them by the *Calimala*. In organisation
the *Arte della Lana* was capitalist and hierarchic. It
employed many more workers than any other guild,[1] but
it kept them in an entirely subordinate position. The
Masters or capitalists bought and distributed the raw
material and sold the finished product through the Guild.
The dyers and retailers enjoyed certain powers of self-
government, but they worked for fixed wages. The weavers
were domestic piece workers, who often lived in the country,
and found it impossible to combine to raise rates of payment. Even if they had sufficient capital to purchase
raw material they were unable to sell the finished product
except through the guild. Country weavers often had

[1] Villani states that in 1339 30,000 persons out of a population
of 100,000 were engaged in the manufacture of woollen cloth.

mortgaged their farms to the masters and were thus completely in their power. At the bottom of the scale were the unskilled or semi-skilled workers—fullers, wool-carders, soap-boilers, beaters and washers—who worked in shops under strict supervision and were paid very low wages. It followed naturally that a main cause of unrest in Florence was the discontent of the workers who were excluded from both political power and economic control.[1]

The majority of those employed by the *Arti Maggiori* had no rights, only obligations rigidly enforced ; their hours and conditions of work and their rate of wages were fixed by Consuls of the Guilds over whom they had no control. At the same time general conditions of life in Florence quickened their intelligence, and made them critical ; from the end of the thirteenth century they became more and more conscious of their grievances and determined to secure redress. They envied the economic associations of the *Arti Minori*, who, even if they had small political power, had at least retained the right of corporate action. By providing guilds along similar lines, the workers hoped to protect themselves from their masters, not under-standing how completely their industry was dependent on capital. The governing class realised the danger and carefully framed statutes prohibiting all associations of workers. A law of 1338 forbade any assembly of wool workers, even for religious purposes. A general statute of 1324 ran as follows : " Since frequently under pretence of lawfulness, unlawfulness is committed, every league or society of persons, not sanctioned by public authority, is forbidden ; wherefore, we decree that no member of any guild, especially workmen of the *Arte della Lana* . . . may assemble in any place, or make laws and ordinances under any title of brotherhood for any motive or pretence

---

[1] *Vide* an article by Professor Rodolico on " The Struggle for the right of Association in Fourteenth Century Florence " (*History*, October, 1922).

of religion, of funerals or of oblations, without the consent of the Consuls of the Guilds." Rigid restrictions of this kind made revolution the only hope of the proletariate.

Similar conditions of labour do not appear to have existed to any large extent in Germany. German capital was utilised in commerce rather than in industry and German imports were paid for, not by export of manufactures, but by the overland, Baltic and North Sea carrying trade. It is difficult to say why grand industry was slow to develop in Germany. Possibly aristocratic opposition to immigration from the country retarded the growth of urban population and thus limited the supply of labour. Industrial development was obviously very closely connected with the size of the urban population and growth of population was rendered difficult in Germany by the sharp division between town and country. Cologne is the only city in Germany which ranks even in the second class in statistical tables grading the cities of medieval Europe according to density of population. It is also probable that the workshops of Italy and the Netherlands were producing a supply of manufactured goods almost equal to the demand. Handicapped by scarcity of labour, the Germans could not expect to find foreign markets for goods which at first would have been of poorer quality and higher price. Historians, by devoting much space to description of the vigorous life of German craft guilds, seem to distract attention from the comparatively small industrial output of German cities. In reality the two facts are closely connected. In consequence of failure to develop grand industry, local industrial organisations retained their strength, wages were kept at a high level and a large wage-earning proletariate did not appear.[1]

[1] The high standard of living no doubt acted as a check on the growth of population. On the other hand, German miners of Saxony, Bohemia and the Tyrol were a true proletariate, oppressed by low wages, long hours, bad housing, child labour, and the truck system.

Social conflict in Germany was not between the merchant guilds and the proletariate but between the craft guilds and the Patriciate.

4. CONCLUSION

The development of commerce and industry led to a renaissance of urban life in Western Europe and acted as a countercheck to the territorialism of feudal landlords, princes and kings. Town-dwellers soon showed considerable aptitude for politics and began to find their own solutions for problems of administration, justice and legislation. Though fear of competition sometimes distorted their judgment, they had more insight into economic problems than territorial rulers. Commercial intercourse with foreign lands helped to raise standards of living, to spread new ideas and to develop an empirical and critical habit of mind. Consequently in the towns new forms of art grew up and found expression in architecture, painting and literature. Renaissance civilisation is primarily an urban civilisation ; its greatest contributions to art and literature come from the towns. Florence was the centre of this great movement ; by the beginning of the fourteenth century she had already produced the first Renaissance architect of secular buildings, Arnolfo di Cambio ; the first great Renaissance painter, Giotto ; the first modern historian, Villani ; and the first modern poet, Dante. The city was a unit small enough to develop rapidly patriotism, consciousness of individual responsibility and a spirit of emulation, a development which found artistic expression, in a manner unknown in half-organised, half-populated monarchies. The small, compact grouping of populations had also political significance ; it helps to account for the bitterness of party factions and the persistence of the democratic tendency. The sense of individual rights was not swamped by numbers. Personal knowledge and criticism of political leaders and the consciousness of direct responsibility gave citizens of small urban communities a compelling interest in problems of government.

Another result of the development of commerce and industry was the increase of the population of Western Europe and its partial regrouping in urban areas. The general increase in population was probably mainly due to the increase in the extent of land under cultivation, a process going on all over Western Europe between the eleventh and fourteenth centuries and carried out by clearing forests, draining marshes and reclaiming waste. As the population drew away from the starvation margin, it increased in size. In England the population more than doubled between 1086 and 1340, rising from about 1,200,000 to 2,335,000 souls. It has been calculated that the total population of western Europe was twenty million in the fifth century, when the Roman Empire broke up, and sixty million in the fourteenth century just before the Black Death ; about one tenth of the sixty million lived in towns, that is, about six million souls.[1] This urban population was very unequally distributed. Four cities—Palermo, Venice, Florence and Paris—had a population of about 100,000 ; five others— Milan, Genoa, Barcelona, Cologne and London—had a population of about half that size. A larger group, including Bologna, Padua, Ghent, Bruges, Strassburg, Nuremberg, Lübeck and Hamburg, had populations of between 20,000 and 40,000 ; a still more numerous class had of between 6,000 and 20,000 (York, Bristol, Ypres, Antwerp, Augsburg, Frankfort, Zurich and Bâle). By far the greater number of towns had a population of between 800 and 6,000 souls.[2] Although these calculations are very

[1] Cf. the calculation that in 1919 eight per cent. of the population of England were engaged in agriculture.

[2] It is interesting to compare these figures with some rough estimate of populations of Greek cities (fifth century B.C.) and with the English census returns of 1921.

I.   Greater London : 7,476,168.
     Glasgow :   1,034,069.

rough, they are of some value as indications of the effect
of industrial and commercial development. The largest
cities were found in Italy and Flanders, where both commerce and industry were developed on a grand scale.
The demand for labour increased the population and the
large population made labour cheap. Next in size came
the greater German cities, primarily distributing centres,
but with local industries strongly developed. They were
all on the highways of commerce : the largest, Cologne and
Strassburg, were in the Rhineland ; Lübeck and Hamburg
were ports for the trade of the Baltic and North Sea ;
Nuremberg and Ulm lay on the eastern routes from Italy
and profited by the distributing trade to the East as well
as to the West. The lesser German towns were not much
more than stations on trade routes and their industrial
products were almost entirely for local markets. It is thus
possible to divide the cities of Italy, Germany and the
Netherlands into three categories. In the first class were

	Birmingham :	919,444.	
	Liverpool :	803,118.	
II.	Cities of about 200,000 inhabitants :		
	Athens.	(Florence and Venice.	Plymouth.
	Syracuse.	were about half this size)	Cardiff.
III.	Cities with populations between 50,000 and 40,000 :		
	Samos.	Ghent.	Worcester.
	Miletus.	Bruges.	Chester.
	Abdera.	Cologne.	Bedford.
		Milan.	Oxford (57,052).
		Genoa.	Cambridge (59,262).
IV.	Cities with populations between 30,000 and 20,000.		
	Ephesus.	Hamburg.	Salisbury.
	Sparta.	Lübeck.	Hartlepool.
	Argos.	Strassburg.	Shrewsbury.
	Thebes.	Nuremberg.	Kettering.
		Bologna.	Reigate.
		Padua.	
V.	Cities with populations between 10,000 and 4,000.		
	Ypres (10,000).	Stratford-on-Avon (9,391).	
	Frankfort (8,719).	Henley (6,891).	
	Bâle (8,000).	Ripon (8,391).	
	Leipzic (4,000).	Ware (5,949).	

cities whose economic prosperity was based primarily on grand commerce : of these the greatest was Venice ; lesser cities in the same class were Genoa, Pisa, Nuremburg, Strassburg, Cologne and Lübeck. In the second class were cities whose economic prosperity was based primarily on grand industry, distributing their own manufactures in return for foreign commodities ; of these the greatest was Florence ; Bruges and Ghent, though not half as large, by specialising in the woollen industry were able to produce on a large scale. Many other cities of the Netherlands belonged to this group, though they were also important as distributing centres. In the third class were cities whose economic prosperity was based on their situation on trade routes and on their local industries ; most German cities and cities on the commercial highways of Italy and the Alps belonged to this class.

Venice and Florence were the commercial and industrial capitals of western Europe. Their activities were reproduced on a smaller scale by Bruges and Ghent, but access to oriental markets and greater freedom of action gave the Italian cities an immense superiority. A speech made by the Doge Mocenigo to the Venetians in 1420 illustrates the great wealth and resources of the city ; he was warning the citizens that a militarist policy would rob them of their commanding commercial and financial position, which he outlined in a summary of Venetian resources. " I design to include in our estimate all the commerce that Venice, to our knowledge, at present conducts. . . . Every week there come to us from Milan from seventeen to eighteen thousand ducats. . . . All bankers declare that every year the Milanese alone pay us sixteen hundred thousand ducats . . . (the cities of Lombardy buy from us yearly), 90,000 pieces of cloth. These cities send to us 1,558,000 sequins of fine gold. We carry on with Lombardy a commerce worth 28,000,000 ducats. . . . Consider how many vessels this commerce maintains in activity, either in transport to Lombardy or in trade in Syria, Romania, Catalonia, Flanders, Cyprus and Sicily. Venice makes a profit of from 2½ to 3 per cent. on the freight. Note how many people live by this carrying trade ; thousands of families of courtiers, workers and sailors and especially the merchants, whose profit is at least 600,000 ducats. . . . The commerce of Venice puts into circulation every year ten million sequins. . . . You Venetians are the only people to whom land and sea are alike open. You are the canal of all riches ; you provision the whole earth ; all the universe is interested in your prosperity : all the gold of the world comes home to Venice." One is irresistibly reminded of the speech of Pericles—" By the greatness of our city (Athens) all things from all parts of the earth are imported hither ; we enjoy the fruits of all other nations."

Mocenigo's speech shows that the wealth of Venice was due primarily to her commerce and industries. Similar conditions prevailed in Florence and Milan, in the great commercial cities of Germany and in the commercial and industrial cities of the Netherlands. Grand commerce and grand industry were alike dependent on capital ; industry required an abundant supply of labour. These factors were bound to have influence on constitutional development, as the direction of affairs by capitalists seemed essential to their prosperity. Such direction was most easily secured by allowing them to enjoy a monopoly of political power ; if this power was exercised to the disadvantage of craft-guilds and wage-earners the democratic tendency was bound to assert itself in agitation for political control, in spite of the fact that any attack on the capitalists was an economic danger. In small cities, less dependent on capital and on the direction of commercial experts, agitations from below were much more likely to be successful. Thus economic conditions had a direct effect on internal political problems. The wealthier and larger the city, the stronger was the tendency to substitute oligarchy

for democracy ; when oligarchs failed to satisfy their
subjects the city ran the risk either of losing its freedom
or of submitting to a tyrant. A converse axiom also held
good. The smaller and poorer the city, the more effective
was the democratic tendency among the artisan class and
the greater was the probability that the Patriciate would
be forced to broaden the basis of oligarchic government.
It is impossible to observe either of these principles working freely, as they were continually deflected or distorted
by pressure of circumstances, yet they may serve as a
general guide through the labyrinth of urban constitutional development.

CHAPTER III

THE PATRICIATE

THE STRUGGLE FOR EMANCIPATION. THE FORMA-
TION OF THE PATRICIAN OLIGARCHY. THE PATRICIATE
IN ITALY.

1. THE STRUGGLE FOR EMANCIPATION

THROUGHOUT Italy, Germany and the Netherlands, towns grew up either as the result of social
conditions or in consequence of a definite intention
to use the town as an agent of colonisation. Whatever
the originating cause, all towns had certain characteristics
in common, which helped to determine their later political
development. Medieval towns were at first anomalies,
based on privilege; they were isolated from the normal
life of the countryside, granted rights denied to rural
districts and formed into legal islands under some kind
of exceptional jurisdiction. The special status achieved
by the town was the necessary consequence of indifference
to urban life during the formative period of public law : a
public law, which under the name of feudalism recognised
a whole series of private bargains and assigned functions
and status to particular persons based on the extent of
privileges secured. The corporate status desired by towns
ran counter to the general system of private bargains and
obligations ; it involved the discard of marks of vassalage
or serfdom, the creation of free citizens and the formation
of a durable system of self-government. The legal peculi-

arities of urban status were at first determined by practical differences between town and country life. When the settlement round the *burg* or fortress of the overlord was protected by a circuit wall the *faubourg* or suburb began to change into the town. The first urban taxes were often levied to build or maintain fortifications; through this common burden the town was legally as well as geographically separated from the country. The population within the walls was increased by immigrants from the country to whom the town claimed the right to give free status. A market and a mint, from which issued the money for buying and selling, soon appeared and their regulation was undertaken by the leading burghers, who controlled sale and purchase, allotted stalls and sites and punished transgressors of custom. Commercial and industrial needs gave rise to special town customs, rapid legal procedure and a business magistracy. When this stage was reached the overlord found it convenient to treat the town as a legal unit and grant it a special judicial organisation. The customary basis of medieval law made essential the co-operation of the burghers in the administration of justice; to secure this certain townspeople were called upon to act as popular judges: in the Netherlands they were called *échevins*, in Germany *Schöffen*, and in Italy *consules*. At first they were nominated by the overlord; later they were chosen by the burghers and accepted by him: finally they were appointed without the consultation or any outside power. They acquired, by degrees, administrative as well as judicial functions, were identified with the magistracy of the mint and market, and came to represent, not the interests of the overlord, but those of the burgher community. Thus, its walls, personal freedom of denizens, market and civic immunity made the town a detached unit with an incipient political life of its own. It remained necessary to convert the favours and privileges granted by overlords into inalienable rights and to secure *de iure* the judicial and administrative power which had been obtained *de facto.* The task of emancipation was complicated by the irregular status of the town ; victory involved a breach with the territorial overlord, yet it was impossible for the town to maintain itself in isolation. Even the smallest town was not self-sufficing, since it depended on the country round it for its food, its raw material and its market. For this reason emancipation could safely be carried out only by persons who thoroughly understood the necessity of maintaining free intercourse with an economic hinterland.

No important constitutional differences can be traced to the legal authority of different kinds of superiors. The overlord, whether king, bishop or secular prince, exercised his authority through a *burg graf* or bailiff, who governed the town in co-operation with representatives of the burghers. The degree of seignorial control he exerted varied in relation to the preoccupations of the overlord and the vigour and wealth of the burghers. In accordance with local conditions, towns became independent republics, stopped short at local self-government or failed altogether to emancipate themselves. It is, however, possible to discern certain practical differences between the urban policy of ecclesiastical overlords and that of secular princes.

In the early middle ages the secular prince spent most of his life in constant movement throughout his dominions and seldom came into continuous relations with his towns. He recognised their financial value and readily granted them legal status. As his main preoccupations were military and territorial, he was always ready to be complaisant to local interests in return for financial aid. As long as the period of territorial expansion continued, the prince was either too weak or too ambitious to thwart the political or commercial activities of urban communities. Until the process of state formation was complete or almost complete, the towns were able to make bargains with their secular overlords. The degree of emancipation secured by the town was invariably in inverse proportion to the degree of territorial unity achieved by the prince. Italian history illustrates very clearly the direct relation between territorial unity and municipal independence. In Naples and Sicily a strong kingdom of the northern feudal type was founded by the Normans, transmitted to the Hohenstaufen and finally divided between the rival houses of Anjou and Aragon. Within its frontiers the free city or commune was unknown. In the Papal States the Pope, after a long struggle, was able first to arrest the development of municipal independence and then to destroy it altogether. The full growth of the free commune occurred only in the northern half of Italy where Popes, Emperors and Kings were alike unable to exert continuous pressure. Where the social and political development of the town had been allowed to reach a certain stage, conflict with the paramount territorial authority was inevitable.

Theoretically the Emperor was lord of Northern Italy and his delegates were the Counts and Marquises of the provinces. Imperial power was strong enough to prevent the rise of powerful local princes, but too weak to interfere with local varieties of self-government. The subjection of the great nobles left the way clear for those of lower degree. The petty nobility of the *contado* became the only serious rivals of the towns ; they were not rich enough to take advantage of imperial weakness to form principalities along lines similar to those followed by the German nobility. They were further weakened by incessant private warfare among themselves and by the long drawn-out struggle between Guelfs and Ghibellines. Through hatred of the towns and jealousy of the Church, they usually supported the Hohenstaufen cause. After the death of the Emperor Frederick II (1250) and the collapse of Ghibellinism in Italy, they were driven from their estates, which passed to the Guelf nobles and burghers of the cities. The power of the territorial aristocracy of Northern Italy was effectively broken before the end of the thirteenth century.

In Germany and the Netherlands the secular prince continued to grow in power throughout the later middle ages, and, as long as the period of expansion went on, the towns were left free to pursue their own ends. Until the middle of the fourteenth century the energy of the German territorial aristocracy was fully occupied in resisting or supporting the Emperor, extending boundaries and colonising new lands in the north and east. When a sort of territorial balance was achieved in Germany and when the Slav revival checked further expansion eastwards, the princes turned to the task of consolidating and organising their dominion. For the first time they began to regard the towns with jealousy and sought either to recover rights forfeited centuries before or to bring neighbouring imperial cities under their sway. In Germany the struggle for municipal independence was a struggle for survival; emancipation from the secular prince had been achieved without difficulty. In the Netherlands the Counts of Holland, Hainault and Flanders for centuries favoured the towns, granted rights of jurisdiction and administration freely and protected commerce from troublesome neighbours. Their continual need of money made them dependent on the good will of rich merchants, who either lent them money, or, later, guaranteed loans raised from Italian bankers. The burghers, on the other hand, were careful not to refuse the subsidies by means of which they retained their independence. The attitude of the Count of Flanders to his towns is illustrated by the type of civic organisation evolved by them. Twelve or thirteen *échevins* were chosen from the burghers by the Count to act as his judges and as councillors of the commune. In the first half of the thirteenth century these magistrates were appointed annually instead of for life ; they were no longer exclusively nominated by the Count but were chosen by the burghers according to a system of election, more or less complicated. The Count's rights were never entirely lost, but they were little more than nominal until the end of the thirteenth century. The civic constitutions of Flanders may be taken as typical of the harmony between towns and secular princes in the Netherlands. Emancipation had been achieved without serious friction, and in the fourteenth century peace was broken, not by the princes, but by civic factions.

Relations between an ecclesiastical prince and the capital town of his diocese were of an entirely different kind. In the capital town the bishop had a permanent residence : he exerted himself to secure its prosperity and good conduct ; as representative of God and the Emperor, he claimed as a right the obedience of his subjects. It was therefore impossible for him to agree to the delegation of power so readily accepted by the secular prince. Friction was inevitable from the beginning and it was increased by ecclesiastical suspicion of commerce and confusion of it with usury. When the Investiture conflict broke out in the eleventh century and the secular authority of bishops was confounded with simony, the towns were very quick to see their opportunity. In 1077, for example, when the Bishop of Cambrai left the city to receive imperial investiture, the citizens rose in revolt against his ministers and proclaimed a commune. Under the direction of a Hildebrandine priest and the wealthiest merchants of Cambrai, they took oaths of fidelity to the commune and pledged themselves to defend it from a restoration of episcopal authority. Similar revolts took place throughout the Netherlands, the Rhineland and Northern Italy. Gregory VII's attack on the Emperor was made the instrument of the economic and political emancipation of the towns. The revolt against episcopal authority was most serious in Italy where the policy of granting temporal power over towns to bishops had been established by Otto I.[1] Many cities in Lombardy and central Italy were governed by bishops from the middle of the tenth until sometime in the twelfth century. Pisa, for example, was governed by her Archbishop and consuls until about 1150 ; Siena emancipated herself between 1137 and 1170 by driving into exile the bishop who had excommunicated her consuls. In Florence the first sign of communal independence can be seen in the revolts (1063–8) against the Bishop, Mezzabarba, who was accused of simony. Milan provides us with the most striking example of the struggle between the bishop and the rising communal authority. The archbishop was the wealthiest ecclesiastic in Italy and by the end of the ninth century he had fortified Milan, established jurisdiction within its walls, and presided over sessions of the Parlamento. A century later the archbishop nominated the city magistrates and entirely superseded the authority of the count. When Conrad VII came to Lombardy (1026) Archbishop Aribert at first supported him and made the war against the cities a pretext for subduing Lodi and Cremona and oppressing the townspeople and the petty nobility of the countryside. A general revolt against his authority broke out in 1035 and, though a reconciliation was brought about in 1044, episcopal authority was not restored.

The Archbishop lost control over Milan and other cities of his metropolitan district until the rise of the Visconti in the last quarter of the thirteenth century. The cities of Italy thus took advantage of the struggle between the Empire and the Papacy to shake off episcopal authority. As the temporal power of the bishops was derived from the Emperor, the cities were usually papalist and Guelf until they had won their freedom. Even in districts where imperial authority had never been strong, the bishops were

[1] Diet of Verona, 967.

driven from power and the free commune of citizens undertook the whole business of government.

North of the Alps conditions were less favourable to the complete emancipation of the cities and a series of compromises was reached by means of which the bishop retained considerable political influence. Usually he continued to draw revenues from the city and to exercise certain advisory powers, though on all important matters the citizens gained control. The chief cities of the Rhineland—Bâle, Strassburg, Spires, Worms and Cologne—remained episcopal residences while rejecting episcopal authority. Two episodes in the history of Cologne illustrate the methods of emancipation adopted by the cities. Lambert of Hersfeld has left the following account of a revolt in 1074: " The Archbishop spent Easter in Cologne, with his friend the bishop of Munster. When the bishop was ready to go home, the Archbishop ordered his servants to prepare a boat for him. They found a good boat which belonged to a rich merchant of the city, demanded it for the Archbishop's use, and threw out all the merchandise with which it was loaded. The merchant's servants resisted. . . . The merchant had a son who was both strong and courageous. He was related to the Patricians of the city and because of his character, was very popular. He hastily collected his servants and . . . the young men of the city . . ., rushed to the boat . . . and violently ejected the servants of the Archbishop. . . . The friends of both parties seized their arms. . . . The riot in the city was finally quieted a little, but the young man, who was very angry as well as elated over his first success, kept on making all the disturbance he could. He went about the city making speeches to the people about the harsh government of the Archbishop and accused him of laying unjust burdens on the people, of depriving innocent persons of their property and of insulting honourable citizens. . . . It was not difficult for him to raise a mob. . . . Besides, all regarded it as a great and glorious deed of the people of Worms that they had driven out their bishop. And since they were more numerous and wealthy than the people of Worms . . . it seemed a disgrace to submit . . . to the rule of the Archbishop, who was governing them in a tyrannical manner. . . ." This passage illustrates the way in which the Patriciate or merchant class took the lead in rebellion against episcopal authority and shows how in Cologne and elsewhere the bishops were unable to maintain their rights of requisition and other prerogatives. A second quarrel broke out in Cologne about the year 1258 between the Archbishop Conrad of Hochstaden and the *Burgermeister*. The Archbishop complained that in former times the *Schöffen*, (popular judges and administrators), had governed the city with his consent : now the burghers, without his knowledge, elected persons to membership of the *Stadtrat* (Town Council), who took oaths of fidelity neither to the city nor to the Church. This *Stadtrat* controlled the whole administration, including finance, encroached upon spiritual jurisdiction, erected gallows and block, taxed the merchants and the guilds and usurped episcopal rights. The elective *Stadtrat* was plainly an innovation, resented by the Archbishop. In order to overthrow it he called in the support of the craft guilds and succeeded in establishing a constitution of a democratic kind. Within a year after his death the Patrician merchants recovered power and put an end to episcopal control. The cities of the diocese of Liège evolved a form of municipal government which is an example of the kind of compromise reached by bishops and their cities in Germany and the Netherlands. Strong episcopal government of a patriarchal kind had been established in the diocese by the end of the tenth century. Though it was popular in the rural districts, it became more and more hateful to the growing towns of the Meuse basin. Between 1066 and 1274 the towns were in a state of chronic revolt against the Bishop, "The solution discovered was a sort of compromise between the prerogatives of the prince and the tendency of the communes to complete autonomy."[1] The towns were granted all rights and privileges necessary for economic development, while the Bishop asserted his authority by retaining control over their judicial tribunal. This tribunal was composed of *échevins*, (twelve in Liège and seven in the other towns), who were appointed by the Bishop for life from the community of the city. All share in the administration of public business was refused to the *échevins* and fell into the hands of a sworn council, (*jurés*), elected by the citizens to look after communal interests. The *jurés* appeared in every town at the time of a revolt against episcopal rule and, though the bishops denounced them as an illegal innovation, they ultimately became a permanent institution. The *échevins* were not finally expelled from the Council until the fourteenth century and they continued to administer justice in the name of the bishop until the end of the middle ages. The compromise of Liège took the form of a clear distinction between a judicature controlled by the bishop and a legislature and executive in the hands of the burghers.

At the critical period of their growth the cities of Italy, Germany and the Netherlands were able either to emancipate themselves from their local overlords or to achieve a compromise which left them free to manage their own affairs. In Italy and Germany the legal status of the Pope and of the Emperor raised a second series of conflicts ; cities which had successfully escaped from the control of local overlords found themselves faced by suzerains with wider claims based on a solid foundation of public law. The resources at the disposal of either Pope or Emperor were more than sufficient to overcome the resistance of any one city. That the cities were able to survive was

[1] H. Pirenne : *Belgian Democracy*, p. 62.

due to the preoccupations of their suzerains and to leagues of defence organised on a federal basis.[1]

2. The Formation of the Patrician Oligarchy

The work of emancipation was undertaken and carried out by those citizens whose wealth and experience had qualified them for office under their overlords. During the process a Patriciate or ruling class arose who gradually secured the monopoly of political power ; under its direction the constitution of the city developed from democracy, through plutocracy, to oligarchy. Democracy was what Plato calls the " Mother form " of the civic constitution. The binding force of popular custom and the struggle for survival united citizens in the discharge of common duties and for the security of the common welfare. Though little is known about early democratic machinery it can hardly be doubted that suitors in the civic courts gave decisions in accordance with popular custom. Magistrates were deemed to be mere agents of the citizens and the mass meeting, *Volksammlung, Concio* or *Parlamento* exercised a direct control over urban government. In the face of common dangers, both political and economic, it was natural to entrust the direction of government to the most enterprising, wealthy and influential members of the community : they became the public officials of the town ; *échevins* in the Netherlands, *Schöffen* in Germany and *Consules* in Italy. They were the link between the town and its overlord and usually the chief agents of emancipation. Their power was due primarily to wealth and was increased either by their possession of land or by the strength of their guild organisations. The gradual process of class differentiation tended to separate these magistrates, drawn from the merchants and landowners, from the artisans and wage-earners of the town. The

[1] For a discussion of the struggle between the cities and the Empire and Papacy see Part II, chapters vi.–viii.

class or estate of merchants and landlords gradually assumed
the monopoly of political power and their Council began to
supplant the mass meeting of citizens. This new Council
—called *Jurés* in the Netherlands, *Stadtrat* in Germany
and *Consiglio* in Italy—was the organ of plutocratic
government. Its general tendency was towards exclusive-
ness. It attempted to shut its doors on new comers, to
make membership hereditary and gradually to concentrate
power in the hands of a few families. Where the process
was completed the government became an oligarchy. A
general political adjustment of this kind went on throughout
the towns of Italy, Germany and the Netherlands. As
Pirenne remarks, " the inevitableness of the change is
proved by its universality." The process may be illustrated
by a brief survey of the early constitutional development
of Zurich, Lübeck and Venice.

Zurich was built on the river Limmat at the point where
it enters the Lake of Zurich. It became an imperial city
in 1218; the imperial bailiff or advocate was a citizen
chosen from the knights of Zurich. From this starting
point a system of autonomous government was developed.
The *Rat* or Council was elected by the citizens and acquired
full judicial, legislative and executive authority. In the
legal code of the city (*Richtebrief der Burger von Zurich*,[1]
1304) the *Rat* appears as the source of authority with unlimited judicial and executive power. It was controlled
by a Patrician caste, composed of the landowning and merchant families of the city. The importance of the landlord
element made the Patriciate more of an aristocracy than a
plutocracy ; many of its members bore hereditary titles
and others, on account of their wealth or services had
received orders of knighthood from foreign rulers. The

[1] The *Richtebrief* dealt with civil and criminal law, the law of
corporations, relations with the Emperor and the composition and
powers of the *Rat*. It has been called " the formal expression of a
free community, autonomous in its domestic affairs."

whole body was organised in a single guild called the *Contafle*, a word derived from the feudal office of Constable and used to show the aristocratic character of the guild. In the fourteenth century complaints against Patrician government became frequent. The *Rat* was accused of maladministration of justice and finance and contempt for the interests of the industrial guilds. The population of the city was small—between ten and eleven thousand—and the Patriciate was unable to resist pressure from below. In 1337 their political monopoly was recalled and a constitution of a less oligarchic kind was substituted.

The internal political development of Lübeck was encouraged by the fact that it was granted many liberties by Henry the Lion in 1181 and became an imperial city in 1226. There was no local prince strong enough to threaten its liberties and the bishop had no temporal power. During the reign of Frederick II the city shook off the control of the imperial bailiff. Henry the Lion had established in both Lübeck and Brunswick a *Stadtrat* of burghers to govern the city. This institution did not appear in Germany before the second half of the twelfth century; its members were known as *Ratmänner* (council men) or *consules*. A twelfth century ordinance states the qualifications necessary for membership of the *Stadtrat* in Lübeck; *Ratmänner* must be personally free, German by birth and directly interested in the prosperity of the city. Any person who had acquired his wealth in an industrial occupation was disqualified for membership. Exclusion of artisans, or members of craft guilds became a fixed rule of the Lübeck constitution. The prosperity of the city depended on commerce; its rulers were the merchants and wealthy burghers, who financed and organised commercial enterprises. *Ratmänner* were elected for two or three years; those who had served their term became life members of a body called the *Alt Rat* and were consulted on important business. The method of appointment to the *Stadtrat* is obscure, but as membership was limited to the Patriciate, popular election was probably soon replaced by co-optation. The Patriciate was not organised in a single *Hansa* or Guild Merchant, but in several companies or colleges of merchants and seafarers.[1] By the middle of the thirteenth century the patrician *Stadtrat* had acquired full control of the mint and the administration of justice in the city. Judicial authority was exercised by the *Stadtrat* and two *Ratmänner* appointed by the *Stadtrat*. Legislation and control of finance were also vested in the *Stadtrat*. Executive power was exercised by officials appointed yearly. In 1298 the most important public officials of Lübeck were two burgomasters, a Chamberlain, a wine master, the *Stadtvogt* or bailiff, two masters of the Market and a *Weddemeister* or controller of industry. Thus the government of Lübeck was entirely in the hands of a plutocracy and the Craftsguilds or *Ämter* were excluded from political control. This political monopoly was regarded as a usurpation of power. In 1340 it was proved in a lawsuit in the papal curia that the final decision in important matters did not lie with the *Stadtrat* but with the whole community. In practice no consultations of the kind took place and, in spite of a series of popular revolts at the end of the fourteenth century, Lübeck remained under the control of a *Stadtrat* of patricians. The *Stadtrat* of Lübeck may be taken as typical of many governing bodies of German cities in the thirteenth and fourteenth centuries. The *Rat* was a plutocratic institution; its members were persons who had inherited or acquired wealth and exercised a controlling influence on the economic life of the city. Political control was vested in a narrow circle of families from whom *Ratmänner* were co-opted. These families were actually a Patrician oligarchy, though not always recognised as such by the laws and constitution of the city.

Venice may be regarded as the arch type of oligarchic

[1] Cf. *Arti Maggiori* or Seven Greater Guilds of Florence.

government. Its full development was mainly due to its geographical situation, its detachment from Italian politics and its early concentration on maritime commerce. Venice, at the extreme east of the Lombard plain and protected by the lagoons, lay off the direct routes from northern Europe to Rome ; it was easy for her to play a neutral part in the continual wars between Guelfs and Ghibellines and to maintain independence from the control of imperial or papal authority. The early development of commerce caused the rise of a rich merchant class, determined to concentrate political power in their own hands and to resist all attempts to establish either a tyranny or a democracy. Their control of the capital and commercial experience essential to the prosperity of the city made it impossible to deprive them of power. During the first centuries of Venetian history political power was nominally vested in the citizens and actually exercised by the Doge. In the twelfth century the merchant aristocracy began to develop the constitution along lines which at the same time deprived the mass of citizens of all political powers and reduced the Doge to the position of a prince who reigned but did not govern. About the year 1172 a Great Council, composed of 480 magnates, was substituted for the *Concio*, *Parlamento* or popular assembly. Soon afterwards all executive power began to be vested in the Doge and his Cabinet. In the first half of the thirteenth century (*c.* 1223) an Upper House or Senate appeared, consisting of 120 members of the Great Council and all magistrates or important officials. The functions of the Senate were primarily legislative ; a scientific legislative system was evolved by making full use of the expert knowledge of officials and magistrates. Elaborate rules of procedure restricted the right of debate to experts and made it possible to deal with much business with remarkable economy of time and precision of method. Judicial business was dealt with by the tribunal or Council of Forty (established *c.*

1187) and was composed of forty members of the Great
Council. The executive organ of the constitution was the
Collegio or administration, consisting of the Doge and
twenty-six heads of departments. The *Collegio* initiated
legislation in the Senate and supervised the execution of
the law. The Little Council was established about 1178 to
curb the power of the Doge ; it was composed of six councillors who were bound to guard against any attempt at
personal aggrandisement by the Doge. They formed a sort
of executive Cabinet. The President of the Little Council,
the *Collegio* and the whole Republic was the Doge. During the early history of Venice he had exercised almost
despotic power and the office was almost hereditary in
certain families. From the end of the twelfth century his
office steadily declined in importance. His personal
authority was first controlled and then crushed by the
merchant oligarchy.[1] Though all acts of government continued to be exercised in his name, he became a ceremonial
rather than a constitutional officer ; he lost nearly all
personal authority and survived as little more than a symbol
of the splendour and power of the Venetian Republic.
This dual movement of the Patriciate against the Doge and
against popular government was brought to completion
between the years 1297 and 1310. In 1297 the Great
Council was permanently closed to the people ; membership was limited to descendants of existing members, and
in 1315 a list of all who were eligible for election was compiled. The privileges and responsibilities of government
were thus confined to a group of about two hundred families.
Finally in the year 1310 an Executive Council of ten was
set up, which was, in fact, a delegation of the power of the

[1] The method of electing a Doge was fixed in 1268. The right
of election belonged to forty-one members of the Great Council,
chosen by an elaborate procedure which involved four series of
voting and seven drawings of lots. A minimum of twenty-one
votes was necessary to elect a Doge. Cf. the two-thirds majority
necessary for the election of a Pope.

Great Council to a still narrower oligarchy. The Council of Ten was at first intended as a temporary substitute for the Senate in times of emergency when haste and secrecy were necessary. Gradually a great deal of legislative and judicial business became concentrated in its hands; in times of war it became the controlling power in the Republic. Members of the Ten were elected in the Great Council for one year only; they transacted business in co-operation with the Doge and Little Council; their chief duty was to receive and enquire into secret denunciations. The Council of Ten, devised at first for emergencies, became, in function, not unlike the Privy Council under the Tudors.[1] It was not an arbitrary or tyrannous institution because its members were elected by the Great Council, held office only for a year and were strictly bound to follow a fixed procedure in co-operation with the Little Council. After its creation the Venetian constitution developed no further, though numerous changes in detail and in procedure were introduced from time to time to make government more efficient and the oligarchy more formidable. In constitutional development Venice seemed to be balanced at a point halfway between monarchy and popular government; the balance was so sure and delicate that the Doge never became a tyrant and the Councils never became democratic.

Venice, Lübeck and Zurich provide us with examples of types of Patrician constitutions which grew up between the twelfth and the fourteenth centuries. Zurich with its small population and comparatively poor Patriciate is typical of the lesser cities of Germany; Lübeck, whose prosperity depended upon capitalistic commerce, represents the form of government evolved in the cities of the

---

[1] The Council of Ten owed its origin to anxiety caused by the Tiepolo conspiracy, (1309), and attempt to overthrow the merchant oligarchy. It was made a permanent institution in 1335.

Netherlands and the larger and wealthier cities of Germany : Venice, owing to specially favourable political and economic conditions, was the archetype of oligarchic government. Each example illustrates the general proposition that the constitutional development of the medieval city was the work of the Patriciate.

The form of oligarchy developed by the medieval city was a remarkable contrast to the aristocratic or feudal oligarchies of national kingdoms. In England, for example, the growth of the constitution was mainly due to pressure brought to bear on the monarchy by nobles ; they attempted to limit the royal power by developing and strengthening legislative institutions. The weakness of the system lay in the indifference of the nobles to the actual business of government. They were content to leave executive authority with the monarch, though they constantly quarrelled with him over the manner in which he exercised it. The oligarchic constitution of the city knew no such division of powers, for the whole energy of the Patriciate was concentrated on the business of government. The importance of economic policy and the small size of the civic unit made impossible the purely spasmodic interest in politics which was the main characteristic of a territorial aristocracy. The merchant or industrial oligarch sought power for economic reasons and continued to exercise it energetically because it was the guarantee of his financial stability. It is not surprising that, within certain limits, he showed political capacity far superior to that of the baron or knight of the shire. He had a direct return for his labour ; he was able to see that administrative business and the direction of foreign and domestic policy were always relevant to his own prosperity ; he did not grudge the time and expense of personal attention to government, because he recognised that by that means alone could efficiency be secured. It is worth remembering that the burgesses of the English House of Commons were the most insignificant members of the national assembly. Unless he could see the direct relation between cause and effect, between expenditure and profit, the municipal oligarch was a failure in politics.

Under the guidance of the Patriciate the constitution of the medieval city developed certain clearly marked characteristics. The Legislative body was active in supplementing customary law by positive enactments. Sometimes, as in Venice, a high degree of legislative efficiency was reached, but more often multiplicity of laws led to confusion and opened a way for incessant disputes in courts of law. Class legislation of a drastic kind pressed hardly on artisans and wage earners. In consequence the Judiciary was weak and overburdened. The common failure to codify custom and statute caused much litigation and made possible perversions of justice in the interests of the governing class. The city state was, normally, too small a social unit to develop a Judiciary, independent of political intrigue and outside the range of influence of a business government. On the other hand, the executive, unlike those of larger medieval communities, was strong and efficient. The ordinary administration was fairly free from corruption and considerable capacity for organisation was shown, especially on the financial side. It is true that the temptation of quick profits sometimes led the Patriciate to take short views of large questions of commercial and industrial policy. The German oligarchs concentrated so much on commerce that they failed to encourage the development of industry; the Florentine and Flemish wool manufacturers helped to ruin themselves by refusing decent conditions of work and wages to their employees. The defects of the patrician executive were due to opportunism rather than neglect or weakness. Its strength at a time of general administrative chaos was the main achievement of the system of government evolved by them.

3. THE PATRICIATE IN ITALY

Oligarchic government along lines already indicated was developed without much difficulty in Germany and in the Netherlands because the Patriciate was united against foreign intervention, against tyranny and against popular government. In Italy, except in Venice, the Patrician class was divided by bitter feuds : in consequence, the normal process of political evolution was interrupted and often deflected from its end. Feuds arose out of divergence of interest between the petty nobility of the *contado* (*Grandi*) and the new merchant plutocracy (*Popolo grasso*). Here the contrast with Germany is remarkable, since the part played by German territorial nobles in the internal government of the town was almost entirely passive. It is true that we read much about the *Geschlechter* or aristocratic families of German cities, especially at the end of the middle ages. Town chroniclers boasted of ancient families who bore coats of arms and whose shields were never hurled back in tournaments; the Teutonic knights admitted to their ranks persons who belonged to the Patriciate of the larger and more important imperial cities.[1] Knights and Patricians together represented the aristocracy (*Adelstand*) of town and country, but it did not follow that the Patricians were *Ritter* who had immigrated to the town. When Charles V was asked to recognise Patrician rank, the petitioners did not base their claim on knightly descent, but on prescriptive right. Urban aristocracy in Germany was a free popular aristocracy, older than the first imperial patent of nobility and running counter to the adage that the Emperor was the sole fount of honour. The cities of Germany evolved their own *Geschlechter* ; in Italy the *Grandi*

[1] " Patriziat oder ratsfähigen Geschlechter der grösseren und angeseheneren deutschen Reichsstädte sind dem stiftsfähigen ausländischen deutschen Adel gleich zu halten," *Instruction für die Legung der 'Ahnensprobe bei dem Deutschen Ritter-Orden,* 24. (Vienna, 1902.)

were an alien caste, immigrants from the *contado*. Some examination of the effect of this migration must be undertaken before the schism in the Italian Patriciate can be understood.

Unlike cities north of the Alps, the population of Italian cities was not homogeneous, either in race or in economic purpose. New elements had been brought into Italian life by the barbarian invasions, elements which help to explain the lack of cohesion in the communes. Though the invaders lost their language and other superficial Teutonic characteristics, they retained the northern belief in territorial organisation on a basis of military service and they were hostile to new ideas of commerce and commercial government on business lines. When the greater nobles disappeared, (twelfth century), the lesser nobles were drawn by centripetal attraction to the cities. Sometimes they came of their own free will ; sometimes the cities were strong enough to compel them to submit to communal officers, to build palaces within the walls and to reside in them for a specified term every year. Whether they were invited or compelled to become citizens, they were soon a powerful influence in the government of the city. They composed the feudal cavalry of the commune and, at first, were the chief means by which cities increased their territory and defended themselves against foreign invaders.

The outward sign of the migration of a military class to the city was the substitution of the private or family tower for the feudal castle.[1] A noble family lived together in the same quarter of the city—often round a small piazza—and protected themselves from their neighbours by erecting a lofty, fortified tower. These family groups were known as Tower Clubs (*Societas delle torre*) or *Consorterie Gentilizie*. The expense of fortification and maintenance was shared

---

[1] Cf. England, where the military class continued to live in the country ; as a consequence the feudal castle dominated rural districts and the towns had no military history.

among the group; the tower was their joint property and no share in it could be bequeathed to any outside person nor any new member elected without the consent of the whole body.[1] Sometimes the tower was let or hired and sometimes payment was accepted for remaining neutral in a local feud. The tower was usually plainly built in brick or stone on a square base; its walls were pierced with openings and on the top engines were placed for hurling stones or throwing fire. Tower, often rose to a height of two hundred feet and sometimes several of them were connected by bridges or galleries. Towers of this kind probably appeared first in the Lombard communes;[2] Pavia was known as the City of a Hundred Towers, Bologna once had a hundred and eighty and Verona claimed to have had seven hundred. Tuscany probably surpassed all other parts of Italy in the number of her towers. A visitor to Pisa in 1154 asserted that he had seen ten thousand towers used both for defence against strangers and for civic warfare.[3] Lucca claimed to have had seven hundred, Prato sixty and S. Gimignano over three hundred, eleven of which are still standing. The private tower and the fortified town house were the outward sign of Italian civic factions. Venice had no private towers and the houses of her merchant princes were built as places of residence, not as fortresses. The contrast between the domestic architecture of Venice and that of other Italian cities can still be observed and serves to remind us of the absence of militant *Grandi* in Venice and, consequently, of the absence of the spirit of faction which was fatal to the independence of nearly all Italian communes.

The *Grandi* as a class retained certain strongly marked

[1] One dissentient vote was permitted.

[2] Similar towers were built in the south of France, especially in Toulouse and the cities of Provence. Louis VIII is said to have destroyed 300 at Avignon in 1226.

[3] Benjamin of Tudela. Of course the number cannot be taken literally.

5

characteristics, which were accentuated by their struggle with the *Popolani*, and by the fact that, like many conservative groups, they tended to be dominated at times of crisis by the most reactionary members of their party. Their military training helped to foster a contempt for civilians, though they themselves hardly came under the influence of the rise of chivalry in northern Europe. Dante wrote of the decay of chivalry (*cortesia*) and ascribed it to the strife brought to Italy by Frederick II. It is more probable that the survival of kindred solidarity among the *Grandi* and the ferocity with which blood feuds were waged checked its Italian development. The *Grandi* were soldiers of such ruthlessness that the refusal of Farinata degli Uberti to allow his men to rase Florence to the ground was regarded as marvellous by his contemporaries.[1] Another dominating characteristic of the *Grandi* was their pride, a quality which helps to explain the vigour of resistance constantly offered to all foreign enemies. It was also the most frequent occasion of private war, which explains why chroniclers so often asserted that personal quarrels were the origin and sole cause of party divisions. The origin of the factions of Black and White Guelfs, which nearly destroyed Florence at the end of the thirteenth century, is traced by ancient writers to a squabble between children, which led to the mutilation of one child and the murder of his father. The pride of the *Grandi* was certainly " one of the most active causes of political effervescence " and was the chief reason why they retained for so long their habits of violence and earned the hatred of the *Popolani*. The same pride made them bad citizens, fundamentally hostile to the idea of the state. They could not endure any distribution of power nor admit that they were bound to obey the law and pay taxes like other members of the community. They

---

[1] Dante (*Inferno*, **X** ,91-2) puts into his mouth the words :—" I was alone when all consented to extirpate Florence, I alone with open face defended her."

showed their contempt for the *Popolani* by calling them
dogs and asses; the *Popolani* retorted by calling them
wolves.[1] The reluctance of the *Grandi* to acquiesce in the
régime of the *Popolo* was also partly due to antagonism
between their ideas of feudal and family organisation and
the popular movement for a government on capitalist
lines. The best men of the aristocratic party distrusted
the new wealth and new ambitions of the bourgeoisie.
Dante believed that " riches are vile " and regretted by-
gone days of narrow means and simple habits. The public
virtues he admired were magnanimity and courtesy; like
S. Francis, he denounced *avarizia* and had only contempt
for the commercial and industrial progress of his native
city. The *nuova gente*, whom he denounces, were the members of the *Arti Maggiori* who were building up fortunes by
means of the wool, silk and corn trade, by banking and by
usurious loans to the *Grandi* who mortgaged their estates
to indulge in the new fashion for building and luxury.
Such ideas were supported mainly by Ghibellines or white
Guelfs. More practical *Grandi* were prepared to make the
best of new conditions, enter the Guilds and discard their
former military habits. By the end of the thirteenth century Tower Clubs were discredited and less warlike forms
of association took their place. The *milites* of Siena were
organised in *contrade* or regional divisions of the city; in
Florence a formidable party organisation grew up under
the name of the *Parte Guelfa* (1267). In spite of the wealth
in land, political influence and military strength of the
nobles their cause was lost once their members began to
desert to the *Popolani*. If they had held together, they
might have been able to establish in the communes an

---

[1] Campagni (III, 2) describes how in 1304 Corso Donati " conspired
with the *Grandi*, pointing out how in many ways they were prisoners
and slaves of a set of bloated *popolani*, or rather, a set of dogs, who
lorded it over them and took the offices for themselves; and by
speaking thus he drew together all the *Grandi* who felt themselves
aggrieved and they made a conspiracy together."

aristocratic form of government, organised on regional or
territorial lines. Had they succeeded, they might have
avoided the schism between town and country which was
the main cause of the military weakness of Italy.

The struggle between *Grandi* and *Popolani* was the main
cause of the precocious development of Italian factions.
In Germany party strife did not appear until the rule of
the Patriciate was challenged by the guilds ; in Italy, at
the critical stage in the evolution of oligarchic government,
the ruling class was split in two and each division tried to
bring the *popolo minuto* into dependent alliance with itself.
By this means the whole community was infected by the
habits of faction and party strife. These factions were
not in themselves a danger ; they were, in fact, often a
sign of life and energy. The appearance of groups of persons who claim to exert a controlling power over the government is inevitable in every society that has reached a
certain stage. In kingdoms the controlling power usually
lay with the Court party or group of persons associated
with the monarch in government. In republics, on the
other hand, the sovereign power of the people was seldom
more than a political abstraction ; effective power was held
in the hands of the party dominant in the community ;
stability of government was in direct proportion to the
preponderance of that party over all others. When two
parties were strong enough to counterbalance each other
more or less exactly, the conflict could usually be terminated
only by a revolution or civil war which destroyed the balance of political power and made one party paramount. In
Italy the balance of parties frequently brought about crises
of this kind. The party in office was forced to adopt a policy
of violence, using measures of disfranchisement and exile
which increased the cleavage between factions and influ-
enced their forms of organisation. Each party developed
characteristic institutions which often amounted to a revolutionary system of defence given permanent form. The

peculiar structure of the commune—" a mere truss of private associations loosely bound together "—gave the strength of party special significance. Nearly all citizens were members of associations which had a more direct claim on their loyalty than the commune itself. The *Grandi* were members of *Consorterie* ; the *Popolani* belonged to *Arti* or guilds ; the clergy were often members of religious corporations. The relation of the citizen to the commune tended to be indirect and through the group to which he belonged, and it was inevitable that the commune should attempt to shake off the yoke of the associations and establish its power directly over all citizens.[1] As the commune was itself merely a mature form of a successful private association, its relations with similar groups were necessarily delicate. The commune strove to break up or render impotent the associations and to centralise power in the name of discipline and the common good ; the associations aimed at absorbing the commune itself or at reducing it to a mere federal band uniting a syndicate of guilds. The whole issue was complicated by the identity of many of the corporations with party groups ; to attack a corporation was to attack a party and thus to precipitate a civic revolution.

Here we find an explanation of the remarkable cleavage between commune and *Popolo* which occurred in nearly all Italian communes. In the twelfth century the word *Popolo* meant the *consortio civitatis* or sworn association of all citizens : a century later it meant an organisation of the people, usually hostile to the communal government. The bourgeoisie or *Popolo*, excluded from or curtailed in the exercise of political power by the *Grandi*, had organised themselves in military and political societies with their own councils, statutes and officers. In many places what

[1] In monarchies the process was relatively simple. In England, for example, the king stood outside and above all corporate groups. The Tudors were even strong enough to assert control over the greatest of all corporations—the Church.

was virtually a secession of the *Popolo* from the commune occurred and the *societas populi* became almost a state within a state. In the battle that raged throughout the greater part of the thirteenth and the early fourteenth century the *Grandi* lost, though the *Popolani* did not always win. In some cities, notably in Florence, the popular leaders joined forces with the most progressive of the nobles and created a formidable oligarchic government.[1] More often the democratic victory was complete and officers of the *Popolani* became first the representatives and then the tyrants of the communes.[2] From the middle of the thirteenth century the continuous defeat of the *Grandi* can be read in statute after statute of the communes. They were deprived of the last vestige of feudal jurisdictions and rights ; they lost the privilege of exemption from taxation in return for military service : their civic rights were rigorously curtailed. They were often specifically excluded from public office and, if politically ambitious, were compelled to renounce their order and enter a guild. The Florentine Ordinances of Justice [3] not only inflicted legal disabilities by imposing on the *Grandi* specially severe penalties for breaches of the peace,[4] but also completely disenfranchised them as a class, Thus the monopoly of political power was secured by the guilds, and the only avenue to public office lay through their organisations. Sixteen years earlier, (1277), in Siena the Council of the Bell.had resolved that only " good merchants of the Guelf

[1] This union between the guilds and the commune, accomplished in 1282 by entrusting supreme authority (*Signoria*) to eight *Priori degli Arti* and confirmed by the Ordinances of Justice in 1293 was the greatest constitutional achievement of the Florentines.

[2] For the details of this process see chapter v. § 2.

[3] Cf. the *Statuta Sacra* of Bologna and the *Libro Rosso* of Perugia.

[4] Compagni thus describes the bitterness of the *Grandi* :—" The Magnates . . . complained loudly of the laws and said to those who carried them out, ' If a horse at full gallop chance to whisk its tail in the face of a man of the people ; or if in a crowd some one pushes another man's chest without intending any harm ; or if little children come to blows, an accusation will be made. . . .'"

party " should be eligible for membership of the Council of Thirty Six, which ruled the city ; the *Grandi*, the artisans and the proletariate were alike excluded from all share in the government. Similar legislation was passed by the *popolo grasso* of Perugia, known as the Raspanti or Clutchers. In 1306 the Great Council of Perugia passed a decree forbidding knights or nobles to enter the communal palace ; in 1333 the names of all the *Grandi* were enrolled in the *Libro Rosso* and it was decreed that members of their families should pay double penalties for breaches of the law.[1] In Florence, Siena and Perugia a new Patriciate arose from the ruins of the old. Though the *Popolani* of many other cities showed the same determination " to treat with virtuous scorn the well-connected," few were able to establish stable government when they had won the victory. Normally, the Italian Patriciate did not long survive the shock of schism and the Renaissance Tyrant emerged from the welter of competing factions which followed the triumph of democracy.

[1] All class legislation against the *Grandi* of Perugia was repealed in 1376.

CHAPTER IV

THE STRUGGLE AGAINST THE PATRICIATE

INTRODUCTORY. FLORENCE AND SIENA. GERMANY.

1. INTRODUCTORY

IN the twelfth and thirteenth centuries municipal government was almost entirely in the hands of a Patriciate of landlords and rich merchants, who were strong enough to maintain urban independence against lay and spiritual princes, to develop a system of administration which gave unity to the city and to carry out a foreign policy adapted to local necessities. In close co-operation with the rest of the citizens, the Patriciate at first aimed at the creation of a self-sufficient economic area, within which each group of workers should contribute a fair share to the sustenance of the whole community. This primitive urban economy was destroyed by the new force of capital, which led to the opening of world markets and the rise of grand industry. As the patrician oligarchies represented the new capitalist class, their interests ceased to be identical with those of their subjects and the old harmony between the various members of urban communities was destroyed. Merchants and captains of industry found that the guild system was a stricture on freedom of economic action and worked to destroy it by breaking down tariffs, releasing merchants from the control of brokers, abolishing fixed prices and generally encouraging the unrestricted activity of individual enterprise.

As a result of their efforts a new element appeared in urban society, a proletariate of wage-earners unprotected by corporate associations and entirely dependent on their capitalist employers. This great economic revolution inevitably had political consequences. From the end of the thirteenth century a double movement against patrician government gathered force. The guilds, jealous for their monopoly rights and critical of the whole foreign and domestic policy of the government, demanded a share of political control. The proletariate, rendered desperate by low wages, bad conditions of work and industrial crises, raised a cry for political rights as well as economic duties and hoped to improve their standard of living by organising themselves in guilds and securing for the guilds political power. The movement swept over the whole of western Europe, taking various forms—peaceful agitations, strikes, riots and even civil war—and lasting for over a century. In England and France the discontent of workers in both town and country found expression in the Peasants' Revolt (1381) and the Jacquerie (1358). In Salonica sailors and artisans maintained for ten years (1342–52) a reign of terror, plundering wealthy manufacturers, landlords and clergy. About the same time the capitalist bourgeoisie of the chief cities of Aragon were forced to give up their monopoly of power and admit the guilds to a share in the government. In Italy the movement was confined to those cities which had retained a free form of government ; it found its fullest expression in Germany and the Netherlands.

The social conflict in the Netherlands has been described with so much learning and art by M. Pirenne, that it is impossible to do more than refer readers to his work.[1] One characteristic of urban constitutions, emphasised by him, has, however, special relevance to the study of German and Italian cities, that is, the constant attempt to adapt

[1] Belgian Democracy. (Translated J. V. Saunders, Manchester University Press, 1915.)

political forms as closely as possible to the economic organisation of the community and thus to secure a balance of
social interests.[1] Like all other attempts to secure a
balance of power, a balance of economic interest was inevitably a continual source of friction. Each economic group
was greedy for power and suspicious of the others ; each
was perpetually demanding a redistribution of public
offices in the hope of increasing its economic control. This
system of distribution of political power in proportion to
the economic interests of groups can be illustrated from the
constitutions of the cities of Flanders, where the monopoly
of the Patriciate was destroyed by a series of popular
revolts at the end of the thirteenth and the beginning of
the fourteenth century. At Ypres the community was
divided into four " members " : (1) the *Poorterie* or capitalist merchants and the butchers, fishmongers, dyers and
shearers : (2) the weavers : (3) the fullers : (4) all other
guilds of artisans. Bruges, a much larger city with a much
more complicated social system, was divided into nine
" members " : (1) the Poorterie : (2) the drapery crafts,
—weavers, fullers, dyers and shearers : (3) the butchers
and fishmongers : (4) metal-working crafts : (5) leather-
working crafts : (6) crafts working with the needle : (7)
the bakers : (8) the brokers and other small crafts : (9)
seventeen other lesser guilds. The government of Ghent,
where the woollen industry was predominant, was organised on lines similar to those of Ypres. The history of its
constitutional experiments illustrates the difficulty of maintaining a balance of economic and political interests.
When the Patriciate was overthrown, (c. 1304), a system
of government by craft guilds was established in which the
guilds were divided into three " members "—weavers,
fullers, and all other guilds—and each " member " was
allotted an equal share of power. An oligarchic reaction

[1] Cf. Industrial representation in the new (1919) German constitution.

came to a head in 1319 and the Patriciate was restored. Eighteen years later, (1337), the guilds again rose in revolt and re-established the constitution of " members," but the arrogance and strength of the weavers were so great that they soon, (1343), deprived the fullers of their third share in the government. In 1349 the weavers were in turn deprived of their share, their place was taken by the *Poorterie* and the fullers were restored. Ten years later, (1359), the weavers supplanted the fullers, who never recovered power. From that time until the destruction of the political privileges of Ghent by the Duke of Burgundy, (1453), Ghent was ruled by three " members," *Poorterie*, weavers and other crafts. Before the economic crisis of the Hundred Years' War and the holocaust of weavers at Roosebeeke, (1382), that is, while community life in Flanders was vigorous, the distribution of political power between " members " caused perpetual discord. If disagreements arose between representatives of the different " members," the minority refused to accept a majority decision ; important questions were either left unsettled or else decided by an appeal to arms. Of the whole system M. Pirenne writes in conclusion : " By carrying to the extreme limit the autonomy of the crafts, long held in check by the patriciate, the government at the same time made friendly relations between them impossible. None of them was ever able to rise above its group interests. It brought to their defence an astonishing heroism, but it was incapable of reconciling them with the interests of other groups. The artisans confused, and could not help confusing, liberty with privilege. Their corporate spirit overcame their patriotism. . . ."

Opposition between rulers and subjects, between " member " and " member " tended to become the predominant factor in urban life. In accordance with the medieval habit of thinking of groups rather than of individuals, the remedy most favoured by opponents of the Patriciate was some form of guild syndicalism. The patrician oligarchs were determined to retain the monopoly of power, on which their private fortunes often depended ; the craft guilds and, less continuously, the proletariate were as determined to wrest it from them. The result varied from country to country and from city to city. Sometimes the Patriciate was forced to surrender control and sometimes it was strong enough to resist all attempts to overthrow it. The craft guilds of some cities were admitted to a share in the government without long conflict and in others they failed to hold political power for any length of time. Nowhere was the proletariate successful in winning a permanent place in the councils of the rich.

2. FLORENCE AND SIENA

Although Italy was disturbed even more than elsewhere by the dislocation of society due to the rise of capital, the struggle against the Patriciate was confined to those cities where a tyranny had not been accepted. The tyrant, by a careful balance of class interests and by the suppression of factions, was able to destroy the political power of the capitalist class. At the same time the democratic tendency was held in check, because craft guilds and wage earners were resigned to a political impotence shared by the nobles and the merchants. In Venice the strong and successful rule of the oligarchy restrained the people from any overt attack on the constitution. Attacks on patrician oligarchies occurred only in those cities where a republican form of government was retained without achieving a balance of the interests of all classes of society. There, attempts were made either to destroy the Patriciate altogether or to establish a mixed constitution in which power was shared between the economic " members " of the community. The movement, though intense, was confined within a narrow circle, almost limited to Tuscany. For our purposes, we will concentrate attention on certain constitutional struggles in Florence and Siena which illustrate attempts to solve two main problems of the medieval city state, the problem of the proletariate and the problem of representation.

Though the great industrial development of Florence throughout provides us with a variety of material for examination of the problems of the proletariate, we will limit attention to the general causes, course and results of the Ciompi Rising in 1378. The *Ciompi* [1] were the proletariate of Florence, the servants of the *Arti Maggiori*, unprotected by any corporate organisation. In 1330 there were already thousands of paupers in the city and their number and misery increased steadily in the next four decades. The long wars of the first half of the fourteenth century had devastated the valleys of the Arno and its tributaries, reduced the productivity of the *contado* and allowed much land to go out of cultivation. A great flood in 1333 and an outbreak of plague followed by famine in 1340 had increased the misery and discontent of the poor. The wars had interrupted commerce and reduced the demand for manufactured goods. A series of banking failures [2] in the forties injured credit and caused trade fluctuations and crises of unemployment. Taxes, especially on food and salt, were high and wages were kept down to the starvation margin. The Black Death, (1348), is said to have reduced the population by half or by three-fifths ; this heavy mortality reacted unfavourably on the conditions of the poor. The general rise in prices was not accompanied by a rise in wages and the scarcity of labour was met by importation of foreigners, who were more easily coerced and had a lower standard of living. Attempts of

---

[1] It is said that the Burgundian followers of the Duke of Athens (1342) called the Florentine poor *compères* or *Ciompi* when inviting them to drink in taverns.

[2] Caused mainly by the outbreak of the Hundred Years' War, (1337), by a run on the Florentine banks in Naples, (1342), and by the failure of Edward III and Robert the Wise to discharge their debts.

the workers to improve their condition were checked by a system of advanced payments which kept them perpetually in debt to their masters,[1] and by severe legislation against all combinations of workers. Strikes and illegal associations to raise wages were a frequent cause of riot.[2]

The complexities of the political situation in Florence seemed to give the *Ciompi* an opportunity to improve their conditions. Since 1343 political power in the city had been divided between the greater and the lesser guilds, but the cleavage of interest between them was so great that the *Ciompi* might well hope to play the part of *tertium gaudens*. The conflict over foreign policy exposed a fundamental difference in attitude. The *Arti Maggiori* were engaged in vast interregional enterprises which involved the republic in the affairs of almost every country in Europe ; they wished to control all the highways and waterways of Tuscany and supported a policy of aggression against the rival cities of Siena, Arezzo and Pisa. The *Arti Minori*, on the other hand, cared little for foreign trade. They grudged the expense and danger of war, but were so jealous of all privilege that they were ready to attack either the Church or the *popolo grasso*. As a result of this sharp cleavage of interest two powerful factions arose in Florence. The patrician faction, led by the Albizzi, consisted of a coalition of the *Grandi* and the *popolo grasso* and was supported by the whole strength of the *Parte Guelfa*. A system of admonitions (*ammonizione*) was developed, by which citizens who opposed the *Parte* were " admonished," that is, formally deprived of all civic rights and, sometimes, driven into exile on a nominal charge of Ghibellinism.[3]

[1] In 1371 a law was passed forbidding wage-earners to pay their debts in money instead of labour.

[2] *Vide* Professor Rodolico's description of two trials of labour agitators in 1343 and 1345 (*History*, October, 1922).

[3] Persons were often " admonished " without accusation or proof. Stefani states that one Captain of the *Parte Guelfa* would say to

By this means persons obnoxious to the *Parte* were excluded from office, and the Patriciate maintained itself in power. Opposed to it was the democratic faction, consisting of the Lesser Guilds, the *ammoniti* and their friends, and supported by ambitious and discontented families of the *popolo grasso*, led by the Medici and the Ricci. The practical issue between the two factions came to be the system of admonitions.

Salvestro di Medici, the leader of the Democratic faction, was elected Gonfalonier of Justice in May, 1378, and thus became Captain of the armed forces of the republic and President of the Priors. He determined to use his right of initiating legislation to destroy the *Parte Guelfa*, being confident that his popularity was so great that the Captains would not dare to admonish him. A compromise was reached and the Captains undertook to " admonish " no one in future who was not really a Ghibelline and to refrain from putting the question of the admonition of the same citizens to the vote more than three times. If the Captains had kept faith, revolution might have been avoided, but before six weeks had elapsed they admonished two citizens against whom accusations had already been rejected twenty-three times. Salvestro immediately brought forward a bill for the total abolition of admonition. When the Priors hesitated to support him he offered his resignation and withdrew from the Palazzo Vecchio. A political dead-lock followed and the craft guilds and *Ciompi* prepared to rise in support of the Gonfalonier (June 18). Terrified by riot and general disaffection, the Priors entreated Salvestro to resume office and to pass the bill abolishing admonitions without further delay. Salvestro

---

another—" Hast thou no enemy ? Consent to admonish mine and I will do the same by thine." Machiavelli states that over 200 citizens were " admonished " between 1356 and 1366 and that every one was terrorised by fear of proscription into honouring the *Parte*. Cf. the expedient of Ostracism used in the Greek city state, though in a much less arbitrary way.

thus secured the political change he desired, but he had entirely underestimated the forces he had brought into play. By stirring up a tumult in the city he precipitated a social revolution.

Encouraged by Salvestro's success and fearing the revenge of the *Parte Guelfa*, the *Ciompi* determined to take advantage of the political crisis to redress their economic grievances and receive a share in the government of the Republic. They realised that they had been used as the catspaw of the democratic faction and would gain nothing by a mere modification of the bourgeois constitution. Belief that they were about to be punished for the riots of June caused them to plan a general conspiracy to overthrow the government. The plot was prematurely discovered to the Priors, but a discussion of measures of repression was overheard by a workman repairing a clock in the *Palazzo Vecchio*, (July 20). He at once carried the news to the working class quarter and in a few hours a vast mob was in arms against the government. The houses of unpopular persons were destroyed. The headquarters of the *Arte della Lana* was attacked and its registers were burned. The Bargello or Palace of the Podesta was seized and a peremptory message was sent to the Priors demanding assent to three petitions. The first petition was from the *Arte Minori* and was primarily political. It demanded the punishment of the Parte Guelfa and the refilling of the purses containing the names of candidates for office. They also requested that a new guild should be formed for the working class population. The second petition came from the workers and demanded the redress of various economic grievances, especially coercion by the officials of the *Arti Maggiori*, indirect taxation and gambling in public stock. They claimed the right to form a working class guild, equal in rights with the other twenty-one. The third petition, also from the *Ciompi*, consisted mainly of demands for the punishment of particular persons.

When the Priors hesitated to accept these terms the *Palazzo Vecchio* was stormed by the mob. The scene has been vividly described by Capponi : " On Tuesday, (July 22nd, 1378), the guilds began to arm . . . and they marched out with their standards. The news was brought to the priors and the Signoria, and they rang the great bell to call a meeting . . . but as the news was spreading the standards of the guilds reached the piazza with the shout *viva populo*. . . . The *Signori* wandered one hither and one thither, one up and one down, and did not know what to do. . . . Then they gave all up for lost ; and . . . they went down the stairs and gave up the keys of the *Palazzo* to the provost of the guilds . . . and went away to their own homes . . . and thus was destroyed . . . the happy, prosperous and tranquil government of the city of Florence. As soon as the *Signori* were gone the gates of the Palazzo were thrown open and the populace rushed in, and one called Michele di Lando, a wool comber or a fore-man in a shop of wool combers and carders, had in his hand a gonfalon, which the people had taken from the house of the *Esecutore di Giustizia*, and he was barelegged, in shoes but without stockings. With the flag he entered the Palazzo at the head of the people and went straight to the audience chamber of the Signory, and there came to a halt. And the people by acclamation gave him the Signory and declared their will that he should be gonfalonier and Lord of Florence."

For a day and a half Michele Lando, the wool comber, was absolute ruler of Florence. At the end of that period he had framed a new constitution for the Republic, prob-ably with the assistance of Salvestro di Medici. The con-stitution of July, 1378, might be taken as showing the high water mark of democratic government in the Middle Ages ; it was not a mere ochlocracy or rule of the mob, but a fair-minded attempt to put an end to class division by granting a share in government to all. Three new guilds were established for the *Ciompi* : (1) The Guild of Dyers, which included most other workers in the woollen industry ; (2) The Guild of Doublet-makers, including tailors, banner makers, hatters and barbers ; (3) The Guild of the *Ciompi*, comprising all those not included in other guilds, chiefly porters and labourers who had no trade, about 9,000 in all. The new constitution distributed political power between the twenty-four guilds. Nine Priors were elected, three from the *Arti Maggiori*, three from the *Arti Minori* and three from the new guilds. Michele Lando was confirmed in office as Gonfalonier and a grant of rents of certain shops was made to Salvestro di Medici. Representatives of the newly enfranchised class were given a share in all public offices. It was hoped that harmony and equilibrium would be permanently established in Florence, as, unlike previous revolutions, there had been no proscription list or violent reprisals to keep factions alive.

In reality, the revolution was doomed to failure from the outset. The *Ciompi* were unfitted for the political power they had acquired and were already out-manœuvred when the new constitution was drafted. They had failed to understand their own situation and made the great blunder of trying to improve it by imitating the political and economic organisation of the upper and middle classes. Their position as wage-earners in capitalist industries was entirely different from that of the artisans and shopkeepers of the *Arti Minori*. The *Ciompi* could not emancipate themselves from their capitalist employers and it was therefore futile to organise themselves in guilds. The whole system of trade corporations was already out of date ; it had been developed for local industry and small scale enterprises : to attempt to force great capitalist organisations, like the *Arti della Lana*, back to the form of primitive equalitarian guilds was to run counter to economic evolution. The plan of government by distribution of power among economic " members " was based on a misconception of the function of capital.

Various practical difficulties also combined to wreck the constitution of the *Ciompi*. Taxation was unpopular and credit was low, yet it was necessary to pay the salaries of public officials and the new civic militia and to give " black rent " to *condottieri* threatening the frontiers of the republic. By the end of August Florence was in danger of famine, as the harvest had been bad and the country population refused to send grain into the city at a time of general insecurity. The landlord class had no sympathy with the new government and were anxious to increase its difficulties. The *Parte Guelfa* and the *Arti Maggiori* were waiting only for a favourable occasion to bring about a counter revolution. They detested the new guilds—" people born yesterday," they called them—and used all negative means at their disposal to bring about a deadlock. Capitalist merchants and manufacturers closed down their workshops —virtually a lock-out—and withdrew to their houses in the country. Thus hundreds of their employees were thrown out of work and the government were powerless to protect them. Many of the *Ciompi* themselves were dissatisfied with the new constitution and believed, with some justice, that Michele Lando had betrayed their cause. He certainly was rewarded with lucrative offices and received a gift of money from the *Signoria*. Certain *Ciompi* thought that more than a third of the public offices should have been allotted to their party in order to make it strong enough to resist a combination of the other two factions against them. They also appear to have been troubled by abstract equalitarian ideas, similar to those preached by John Ball in England before the Peasants' Revolt. Some of them wished for community of goods and the abolition of the whole hierarchy of corporate trades. Attacks from this left wing of the reforming party led to the overthrow of the constitution.

On the 27th August a body of about 5,000 discontented

Ciompi assembled in the piazza of San Marco and drafted a series of radical petitions which they presented to the Priors. In order to ensure their success they set up a provisional government, organised on the lines of the *Parte Guelfa*, and invited the other guilds to send delegates to help them in drafting another new constitution. Their action roused general opposition and the rumour was spread that the *Ciompi* wished to establish a tyranny in Florence. After a few days of futile negotiation, the militia of the guilds was called out against the *Ciompi*, who were routed in a series of street fights and killed without mercy. The banner of the twenty-fourth guild was thrown down from the Palazzo and the twenty-fourth guild was dissolved. The workers were disarmed and large concessions were made to the peasants to dissociate them from the *Ciompi*. A new constitution was devised, which allotted four priors to the *Arti Maggiori* and five to the sixteen other guilds, a division of power proving that the defeat of the *Ciompi* was secured by a coalition of all the guilds against them. During the next four years the *popolo grasso* gradually recovered lost ground. Finally, with the help of foreign mercenaries, they succeeded in suppressing the other two new guilds of dyers and doublet-makers (1382). The *Parte Guelfa* recovered its privileges and the share of the Lesser Guilds in public offices was reduced, first to a third and then to a fourth, (1387). Revolution and counter-revolution had made a full circle and the Florentine constitution was again much as it had been in 1293. The middle class had tried to secure political control by making use of the *Ciompi*; the *Ciompi* in turn had seized the opportunity to claim a share in the government, but were destroyed by a combination of the middle and upper classes against them. In the end the middle classes were crushed by the hired forces of the *popolo grasso*.

The result was the triumph of plutocracy in economics and oligarchy in politics, each in its own way fatal to

Florence. The capitalists of the *popolo grasso* tightened their grip on the workers and gradually crushed out their initiative and interest in affairs. Those who could, emigrated, and the remainder existed in an apathy which reacted on the industrial life of the city. Commercial supremacy, once enjoyed by Florence, passed to national monarchies where the power of capitalist guilds was checked by the Crown. In politics a similar decadence followed. Every year the number of oligarchs became smaller and party politics degenerated into mere family quarrels. Political power passed into the hands of a few families, then to a single family, finally to an individual, Cosimo di Medici. The Florentine solution of the problem of the proletariate helped to prepare the way for the conversion of the republic into a tyranny.

In Siena political conditions were similar to those in Florence, but the merchant plutocracy was just not powerful enough to establish complete dominion. The intense vitality of political life was such that the democratic tendency was not only strong enough to resist the Patriciate, but persistent enough to force the Sienese to reject the facile solution of tyranny and to attempt to solve the problem of representation. An outline sketch of their constitutional history will show how for over three centuries the oligarchic tendency and the democratic tendency pulled against each other and what great efforts were made to find a neutral point between them.

Siena lies in the hill country that forms the southern frontier of Tuscany. Its early importance was due to its position on the main western road to Rome. From the time of Charlemagne pilgrims, coming from the north and west to visit the tombs of the Apostles, landed at Pisa, passed up the Arno valley to Empoli and then, turning due south travelled up the Val d'Elsa to Siena.[1] This road

[1] The *Via Cassia* or Roman road ran north past Lake Trasimene to Arezzo, down the Arno valley to Fiesole and through Pistoja

to Rome was the spine of medieval Tuscany, and all the problems of the province are bound up with its history. When military expeditions of German Emperors began to follow pilgrim bands Siena became the natural base for a descent on Rome. From the eleventh to the thirteenth century Siena dominated the great road and became rich through imperial favours and pilgrim traffic. From the twelfth century merchants of Siena were engaged in commercial and financial undertakings throughout western Europe. Until about 1260 they were the chief bankers to the papal curia and they carried on business as dealers in cloth and money changers in both France and England. The constitution of the city developed along lines very similar to Florence. In the twelfth century government was in the hands of consuls ; in the first half of the thirteenth century a *Podesta* and a Captain of the People appeared as chief officers of the commune. The city was disturbed by the usual struggles between *Grandi* and *Popolani*, culminating in the defeat of the *Grandi* after the Ghibelline disasters of Benevento and Tagliacozzo. A strong merchant Patriciate then established a monopoly of political power. In 1277 it was resolved in the Council of the Bell that only " good merchants of the Guelf party " should be eligible for membership of the Council of Thirty-Six, which governed the City ; nobles, artisans and proletariate were excluded from all share in the government. The governing body decreased in size and came to consist of only nine members ; the merchant class became known as the *Monte* or party of nine.

Domination of Siena by a merchant Patriciate lasted for

and Lucca to the coast. This route was made impassable by the flooding of the Chiana valley between Montepulciano and Arezzo and by the spreading of the Arno marshes. Florence, the chief rival of Siena, lay off the medieval route and was therefore outside direct imperial influence, but as soon as its inter-Italian trade began to develop, her position at the point where the roads across the Appennines to the *Via Æmilia* converge more than outweighed the disadvantage of distance from the highway to Rome.

almost eighty years (1277–1355), but in all that time political stability was never securely established. The main cause of the weakness of the government can be traced to the general decline of the prosperity of the city. Florentine competition injured the Sienese cloth trade and helped to ruin Sienese banking. Papal custom was lost partly on account of the Ghibellinism of the city and partly owing to the success of the gold florin issued by Florence, (1252). The absence of a good water supply checked the growth of industry and the Black Death is said to have caused a mortality of three-quarters of the population. Dissatisfaction with the government, who were blamed for all disasters, caused the formation of factions, representing economic interests and anxious to redistribute political power. The parties opposed to the ruling oligarchy or *Monte Noveschi* were the *Grandi*, including country squires as well as nobles resident in Siena, the *nouveaux riches* or merchants and traders who were excluded from the government and the *popolo minuto* or artisans and wage earners who called themselves the Reformers (*Riformatori*). In 1355 these disfranchised factions seized the opportunity of the presence of the Emperor Charles IV to overthrow the *Monte Noveschi*. Disputes at once arose over the distribution of power. At first authority was vested in a council of twelve *nouveaux riches*, known as the *Dodicini*, which was bound to consult a College of twelve *Grandi* on all important business. The *Dodicini* soon showed themselves to be weaker, more corrupt and at least as neglectful of the common interest as the *Noveschi*. After thirteen years of misgovernment they were driven from power, (Sep. 2, 1368), and a Council of ten *Grandi* and three *Noveschi* was established in their place. The *popolo minuto* were discontented with the new constitution and in less than a month, (Sep. 24), they substituted a governing body from which the *Grandi* were excluded and in which power was divided between three *Noveschi*, four *Dodicini* and five

Riformatori. The *Riformatori* were still dissatisfied and with the help of Malatesta, an imperial general then in the city, forced a third constitution on the city in December, 1368 ; all power was vested in the *popolo minuto*, represented by a Council of fifteen *Riformatori*. Within five days it was clear that the Government rested on too narrow a basis and seven *Riformatori* were dismissed and replaced by four *Dodicini* and three *Noveschi*. After four revolutions in as many months a government, known as the Fifteen Defenders, was established which was a deliberate attempt to put an end to factions by allotting power to each group of economic importance. Even the *Grandi* were allowed to hold certain public offices, though excluded from the Council of Fifteen. The old party names were abolished and replaced by a division of citizens into three categories :—(1) The " people of the least number " or *popolo grasso* : (2) " the people of the middle number " or *nouveaux riches* : (3) " the people of the greatest number " or *popolo minuto*. These " members " were represented in the councils by three, four and seven Defenders, numbers being allotted in direct relation to numerical strength. Thus the constitution of the Fifteen Defenders was, in effect, a crude attempt at proportional representation ; its distribution of political power was the first clear recognition of the power and rights of the majority.

The weakness of the constitution supported by unequally balanced " members " was soon apparent. The old factions continued to disturb the city and political discontent was increased by commercial depression. The woolworkers were in great distress owing to unemployment and low wages. In 1371 they rose in revolt, and expelled the four representatives of the " middle number " from the council, and thus secured for the " people of the greatest number " twelve representatives against the three of the *Noveschi*. Fourteen years later, (1385), an aristocratic revolution destroyed the government of the Fifteen Defenders. A new constitution divided power in new proportions ; the magistracy consisted of four *Noveschi*, four *Dodicini* and two representatives of the *Monte del Popolo* or the fraction of the *popolo minuto* who had not supported the *Riformatori*. The Reformers themselves and about four thousand artisans were expelled from Siena. The city was so disturbed and weakened by faction that it was forced to submit to the overlordship of Gian Galeazzo Visconti. After his death, (1402), further tumults led to the expulsion of the *Dodicini* and the recall of the Reformers. A government was established which consisted of a coalition of the *Noveschi*, the Reformers and the *Monte del Popolo*, each represented in the Signory by three magistrates or Priors. Siena was governed for nearly eighty years under this constitution or some modification of it. In the eighties of the fifteenth century a fresh series of revolutions and expulsions occurred. The Reformers were driven from office in 1480 ; the *Noveschi* were condemned to perpetual banishment in 1482-3 ; the *Noveschi* recovered power under the leadership of Pandolfo Petrucci in 1487. Pandolfo then established what was virtually a tyranny, lasting until his death in 1512. Asked by the Pope by what means Pandolfo maintained his rule in Siena, his secretary replied, " Holy Father, by lies." By fraud rather than by force, Pandolfo governed Siena, but he did not succeed in making any permanent constitutional change. After his death the old faction fighting was resumed. The *Noveschi* were opposed by a new *Monte de Libertini*, who held democratic opinions and posed as the patriotic party. The forms of republican government survived in spite of faction and foreign war for almost half a century. Finally in 1555 Siena, after a heroic siege, was captured by the Spaniards and became part of the Grand Duchy of Tuscany.

The main interest of the bewildering constitutional history of Siena lies in the intense vitality of its political life. The prestige of Florentine historians has helped to impose the legend that Florence was the most democratic and vigorous of the Italian city states. In reality, Florentines lost interest in politics after the Ciompi rising and settled down under an oligarchic constitution which slowly transformed itself into a tyranny. The revival of the republic under Savonarola was little more than a brief fever of religious and patriotic excitement in which constitution-makers and citizens showed that the true democratic tendency was atrophied.[1] In Siena, on the other hand, political energy and the spirit of experiment seemed almost inexhaustible forces. From the middle of the fourteenth century, that is, from the time when either tyranny or oligarchy was triumphant in Italy, the Sienese began a long series of constitutional changes, ever seeking to find a balance of interest which would give them a stable government. No positive result was achieved : the factions were too strong, too hostile to each other and too equally matched to permit any permanent co-operation in government. The interest lies in the persistence of the democratic tendency, rather than in its forms. It is indeed a paradox that the people known throughout Italy as the " soft Sienese " should have proved themselves to be more tenacious of their political rights than the subjects of any other medieval city state.

3. GERMANY

The governing body of a German city was the *Stadt-rat* or Council. Membership of this body was, until the end of the thirteenth century, usually confined to a narrow circle of patrician families, often not more than twelve or fifteen in number. They formed an exclusive social as well as political caste and refused to admit into their *Burgerstube* or aristocratic guilds persons who were not of noble birth or were engaged in industrial occupations. In Lübeck, for example, it was an essential part of the

[1] Cf. chapter v. § 3.

constitution that no artisan should sit in the *Rat*, though *Rat* officials had full control of the regulation of industry. On the whole, these German Patricians were careful guardians of the welfare of their cities, at least until the cleavage of interest caused by the rise of Capital. Then as a commercial nobility—*Handelsadel*—they drew away from the rest of the citizens and began to govern almost exclusively for their own advantage. The artisans were oppressed by indirect taxation, dishonest administration and partial law courts ; they also bitterly resented the insolence and capricious behaviour of the Patricians both in public and private life. The craft guilds claimed that, as their services were essential to the prosperity of the city, they had a right to representation in, if not control of, the *Rat*. They denounced the comparative leisure of the Patriciate as the product of usury and often considered them as little better than Jews. Pogroms of the later Middle Ages, especially at the time of the Black Death, were usually carried out by mobs in defiance of the government and were, probably, a covert attack on the Patriciate. As bitterness increased, the ruling class became more violent in their attempts at repression. In Magdeburg, (1304), ten aldermen of the guilds were burned in the market place—a year later several leaders of the popular party were buried alive in Brussels and in Cologne after the " Weavers Battle " of 1371 over 1,800 weavers with their families were expelled from the city. " White Terror " of this kind was hardly a general characteristic, though its existence proves the width of the schism between the Patriciate and the rest of the citizens.

The democratic tendency was certainly strong in German cities during the later Middle Ages, but it is by no means easy to estimate its full force or to trace its influence on the great number of cities which it disturbed.[1] Some

[1] In the fourteenth century there were about 3,000 towns in Germany.

historians, notably Lamprecht, have found in the urban revolts of the fifteenth century a full programme of social democracy; they understand the object of the risings to have been the abolition of the capitalistic system, the recognition of the sovereign rights of the community with full power of initiative and the reduction of the *Rat* to a mere executive organ of the popular will. Such an interpretation of the facts seems to arise out of confusion, not only of economic causes with political results, but of two phases of social conflict which, though overlapping in time, were quite distinct in character. If the more significant social revolts from the end of the thirteenth to the end of the fifteenth century are examined as a whole, it will be seen that no chronological line of division can be drawn. The disturbances of the fifteenth century were of the same kind as those of the fourteenth century; they were *Zunftekämpfe* or risings of the guilds against the patrician oligarchy. The purpose or results of these *Zunftekämpfe* must not be confused with the sporadic risings of the poor against the rich, of the proletariate and poorer guilds against capitalistic government. Though the proletariate often supported the guilds in the struggle against the Patriciate, the two groups were united by nothing more than a common hatred of the *Geschlechter*. The guild leaders were by no means socialistic and the reforms they sought were purely political and administrative. They wished to substitute *Handwerksadel* for *Handelsadel*, to replace the commercial oligarchs by an oligarchy of industry, or at least bring about a division of political power. Their ultimate object was a change of persons, rather than a change in the whole system of government.

In southern and western Germany, where the craft guilds were closely united and where the Patriciate had not been disproportionately enriched by grand commerce, the *Zunftekämpfe* were usually followed by constitutional change. In some cities, especially in Westphalia, the conflict was never sharp and a more or less friendly compromise between the Patriciate and the guilds was reached. Examination of events in Dortmund throws some light on the manner in which constitutional changes were brought about.[1] Dortmund had grown out of a union of several peasant communities round a royal court ; it owed its early prosperity to its situation on the main road between the Elbe and the Weser.[2] The *Rat* or *Schöffenrat* is first mentioned in 1241 ; the autonomy of the city was established and defined in an electoral ordinance of 1260, according to which membership of the *Rat* was limited to persons elected by the six craft guilds [3] and the Guild of the Blessed Reynold, a patrician guild of *Erbsassen* or hereditary landlords. A change was made, or perhaps merely confirmed, by a charter of liberties granted to Dortmund in 1332 by Lewis of Bavaria which contained the following clause :—" We wish, most strictly enjoin and command as an immutable statute and ordinance, that you shall have a *Rat* of eighteen *Ratmänner* . . . of the better, more ancient and distinguished families (provided that father does not sit with son or brother with brother in the same *Rat*), men legitimately born and honourably married, who shall hold office for life. . . ." Thus political power was limited to a Patriciate of *Erbsassen*. The guilds still retained the right to assist in the election of *Ratmänner* but the number of *Erbsassen* was so small and vacancies occurred so seldom that they had small opportunity for the exercise of a selective vote. As dissatisfaction with the financial and general policy of the Patriciate increased,

---

[1] Cf. Munster, Soest and Osnabrück.

[2] In documents of Otto III, (990–1000), traders of Dortmund were put on an equality with those of Cologne and Mainz.

[3] Tanners and cobblers, bakers, butchers, smiths, dairymen, and shopkeepers. A seventh guild of tailors secured recognition in 1379. Note that these guilds were in no direct way financially dependent on the capital of the Patriciate.

exclusion from the *Rat* became intolerable to the guilds. In 1399 the whole community rose in revolt, abolished the constitution of 1332 and substituted the form of government which had been defined by the electoral ordinance of 1260. That their conservatism was deliberate is shown by the oath imposed on all citizens to maintain the ancient rights of Dortmund against the Emperor and every other power. On the representation of certain creditors of the city, the Emperor Rupert outlawed Dortmund and commanded that the Patrician *Rat* should be restored in accordance with the charter of Lewis of Bavaria, with the addition of six new members representing the whole community. The citizens disliked this settlement and in 1406 secured from Rupert a confirmation of the constitution of 1399. Thus the oligarchy of *Erbsassen* was overthrown and a mixed constitution, in which power was shared between the old Patriciate and the guilds, was established in its place.

The immediate results of the *Zunftekämpfe* varied almost from city to city. Sometimes, as in Frankfort on Main and Halle, the Patriciate retained full representation in the *Rat*, while admitting proxies of the guilds to a share in political power. In other cities the guilds succeeded in forcing the adoption of the guild system of " members " and compelled *Geschlechter* to sit in the *Rat* only as guild representatives.[1] A conflict between the two parties in Constance illustrates resistance to this system. In 1429 the *Rat*, in which the craft guilds had a majority, inflicted heavy fines on certain citizens who had seceded from craft guilds and entered the guild of *Geschlechter* ; all changes of this sort were prohibited for the future. When the *Geschlechter* protested, pleading their rights as citizens, a great tumult against them arose in the city, their lives and property were in danger and they saved themselves only by undertaking to emigrate from Constance to Schaff-

[1] E.g. in Augsburg, Constance and Magdeburg.

hausen. In subsequent negotiations, conducted under foreign arbitration, it became clear that the issue underlying the quarrel was a dispute as to what share each party should have in the composition of the *Rat*. The Emperor Sigismund established peace in 1430 by ordaining that craft guilds and *Geschlechter* should each have a half share.

Nuremberg was an important exception to the general modification of urban constitutions in southern and western Germany. The city was the central point of German commercial distribution ; it had grown up round a castle built by Henry III (*c.* 1050) and the relics of S. Sebald had made it a place of pilgrimage. In 1219 it received a charter from Frederick II, granting full control of administration, police and finance. These powers were exercised by a *Rat*, members of which were at first freely elected by the community. The circle of *ratsfähig* persons gradually decreased in size until only about forty patrician families were eligible for membership. The patriciate of Nuremberg was the greatest urban aristocracy in Germany. Its members had extensive commercial and considerable industrial interests : they wore the dress and carried the arms of knights : their hatchments hung in churches : they were extensive landholders, and, unlike *Geschlechter* elsewhere, they led armed forces to war in defence of their city or their allies. A revolt against their rule broke out in 1348.[1] The guilds and the proletariate complained of the secrecy with which the *Rat* conducted business, of a refusal to allow audit of accounts and of partial administration of justice. Taking advantage of a crisis in imperial politics, the craft guilds called in the support of the Wittelsbach house, expelled the Patriciate from the city and set up a new *Rat* of their own representatives. The new government failed to maintain themselves in power,

---

[1] Few details of the revolt are known. As it was unsuccessful, chroniclers pass it over as a disgraceful episode. The account of Sigmund Meisterlin is mainly rhetorical abuse.

chiefly owing to the passive resistance of the class on whom the prosperity of the city depended. Administration and finance broke down almost altogether. Meisterlin says " all business was at a standstill ; no one had any money ; the public streets were blocked with weeds and thorn bushes." The citizens became so discontented with the new régime that Charles IV restored the Patriciate without difficulty in the following year. Twenty-three guild masters were executed and a hundred banished by royal command. From 1349 onward the government of Nuremberg remained in the hands of the *Geschlechter* and there can be no doubt that the city prospered under their new rule. They undertook large commercial enterprises, were generous patrons of art and learning and built palaces in Brabant and Venice as well as in Nuremberg.[1] As a considerable part of their private fortunes was invested in the public debt of the city, to have overthrown their government would probably have reduced Nuremberg to bankruptcy.[2] Their administration remained good until the seventeenth century, though about a hundred years earlier they began to degenerate into mere jurists and bureaucrats, to live on their incomes and to withdraw from that traffic in foreign markets on which the commercial greatness of Nuremberg was based.

Nuremberg provides us with the closest parallel to the constitutional history of northern German cities, where the Hansa cities were equally dependent for their prosperity on the capitalist enterprises of their *Handelsadel*. The Hanseatic League was a curb to the democratic tendency. For example, when the Patriciate of Brunswick was driven

[1] Of Nuremberg Aeneas Silvius, afterwards Pius II, observed in 1468 : " Private dwelling houses seem to have been built for princes. In truth kings of Scotland would gladly be housed as luxuriously as the ordinary citizens of Nuremberg. . . ."

[2] In 1440 the public debt was in the hands of thirty-one *Ratsfamilien* ; the Halle family drew twelve hundred and the Holzschuber family eight hundred pounds interest from the *Losungsstube* or Finance Office of the city.

from power, (1374), the League outlawed the city and, by crippling its commerce, starved it into surrender.[1] Yet even in the north the shock of the *Zunftekämpfe* was severe. The artisans of Lübeck rose in revolt in 1405 and in 1408 a new *Rat*, admitting guild representatives, was established. In Rostock and Wismar (1409) merchants and craft guilds combined against the oppressive rule of the Patriciate and forced their representatives into the *Rat*. The commercial *Geschlechter* of Hamburg, (1410), were forced to admit sixty citizens into the *Rat*, whose consent was necessary to the business of the Hansa, to declaration of war or to levy of extraordinary taxation. The intervention of the Emperor Sigismund, (1416), was necessary to restore to power the Patriciates of the greatest Hansa cities.

Throughout the later middle ages the hostility of the proletariate to the government remained of secondary importance, as the relatively small population of German cities and their failure to develop grand industry had helped to maintain standards of living and check the growth of a large class of wage earners, casual labourers and beggars. In the fourteenth century, except in Cologne, the discontented poor had seldom any programme of reform and did little more than support the guilds in assaults on the Patriciate and join in pogroms. Conditions began to change in the fifteenth century when the guild system was breaking down and the ascendancy of capital was established. Especially in the cities of northern Germany, a slight, though significant, socialist tendency can be discerned. In Magdeburg, (1402), a popular mob, suspicious of the financial administration of the city, burnt the bishop's mint, attacked the *Rathaus* and looted the market, the richer guild halls and the houses of the clergy. As an aftermath of a political disturbance in Brunswick (1445), the

[1] In the East the *Sechstädtebund* of Upper Lusatia acted in the same way, using its federal power to repress *Zunftekämpfe*.

7

poor guilds of Shroudmakers, Tinkers and Furriers conspired against the *Rat*. The Tinkers, armed with rakes and other weapons, paraded the streets, saying that they would destroy the rich and plant cabbages in their garden, and that, unless the price of beer mugs was reduced enough to allow poor men to be able to buy them, they would break in pieces the kegs in the beer cellars. Plans were laid to behead the *Ratmänner* and slay the rich, but the conspiracy was betrayed to the *Rat*, and the movement was severely repressed.[1] In Hamburg, (1483), a tumult due to purely economic causes broke out, due to famine and the high price of corn at a time when the merchants were shipping grain from the City. The poor were stirred up by the oratory of a demagogue, a brewer or butcher called Heinrich von Lohe. When the *Rat* imprisoned him for creating disaffection he was released by an angry mob, who demanded the death of the ruling class and the distribution of their goods among the poor. The revolt was put down after heavy street fighting and its leaders were executed. The *Rostocker Veide*, (1487–91), was a rising of a similar kind. The combination of Patriciate and middle class against the proletariate was always too strong to allow them more than momentary success, but their risings were symptoms of a growing public danger which finally exploded in the social wars of the Reformation.

The constitutional history of Cologne provides us with a link between the *Zunftekämpfe* and the risings of the proletariate, since in it we can discern the simultaneous action of both movements. The task of emancipation from the power of the Archbishop had been carried out by a Patriciate of merchant capitalists, who formed a business corporation known as the *Richerzecke* and, either directly or indirectly, controlled the commercial and industrial policy of the city. In the middle of the thirteenth century,

---

[1] A second disturbance of the same kind took place in Brunswick, (1488), led by the furrier Ludecke Holland.

(*c.* 1242), an elective *Rat* appeared : it was not a closed patrician council, but a body which, though aristocratic in composition, was elected by the respectable burghers of the city. A curious double constitution had grown up by the first quarter of the fourteenth century. Executive power was exercised by a small body, known as the *Enge Rat* or Little Council and consisting of about fifteen Patricians. For important decrees the consent of the *Weite Rat* or Great Council was necessary. The eighty-two members of the *Weite Rat* were elected annually by the parishes of the city and district ; many of them were Patricians. Though political control was for a time in their hands, the Patriciate were unable to establish a permanent oligarchy in Cologne. They were opposed by the Archbishop, who encouraged the craft guilds in resistance, and threatened by the turbulent industrial proletariate.[1] Patrician government failed to satisfy the citizens, as its general policy was too narrow and selfish to permit free economic development. The ruling class attempted to exclude foreign commercial competition ; they prohibited relations between the craft guilds and the London market, harassed and obstructed the woollen industry and made determined enemies of the Wine Guild, the Brewers and the Butchers. Opposition was organised by the *Wollen Amt*, which included a number of small masters. In the weavers' insurrection of 1370 the guild, supported by the working class, succeeded in substituting a *Rat* of fifty artisans for the *Enge Rat* of fifteen Patricians,[2] An

[1] Cologne, partly through its development of the woollen industry, had a population almost half as large again as any other German city.

[2] Of this change one chronicler wrote : " It was strange and wonderful to behold how Cologne was polluted by such councillors. From the beginning of its existence the city had been ruled by fifteen noble families, descended from the Romans and usually knights of ancient descent, as their shields, never hurled back in tournaments, can prove [*sic*]. The weavers now sat in their places and they made themselves of so much account that the majority

artisan government was obviously unfit to handle the commercial and industrial policy of Cologne and it is not surprising that it lasted for less than a year.[1] The weavers soon showed themselves to be lawless and incompetent : they alienated sober citizens by breaking up courts of justice when attempts were made to punish them for riot. Finally the Patriciate and the guilds combined against them, called out the civic militia and routed them in a series of street fights. The Patriciate cheated their allies by setting up a completely aristocratic form of government. The *Wollen Amt* was suppressed and the other craft guilds were forced to surrender their charters, abandon their guild feasts and sessions and submit to the supervision of two *Obermeister*. Patrician rule thus reached its height in Cologne, but it did not last for much more than twenty years. Without further bloodshed and by making use of the democratic form of the constitution, the Patriciate was turned out of office in 1396. An entirely new constitution was adopted. All political power was vested in the guilds, which were organised in twenty-two corporations, the largest of which was the *Wollen Amt*, and all persons domiciled in the city were bound to become guild members. The twenty-two guilds elected thirty-six Ratmänner ;[2] these thirty-six co-opted thirteen additional members and the total forty-nine became the *Rat* or representative assembly of all citizens. The Patriciate as a ruling class, disappeared and the constitution of Cologne remained the greatest achievement of the democratic

of the *Rat* (*Weite Rat ?*) was on their side." Cf. the sarcastic question of the poet Hagen : " What do fellows understand of government who have been spinning or fishing or baking all their lives and at most know how much a herring is worth ? Ass remains ass even in a lion's hide."

[1] Cf. the Ciompi rising in Florence (1378), and the Nuremberg rising of 1348.

[2] The number of Ratmänner elected by each guild was in proportion to its economic and political status. Cf. the constitutional experiments of Siena.

tendency in the German city state. Even here the oligarchic tendency was ultimately stronger ; the democratic form of *Rat* election did not prevent the rise of a limited number of political families, who were, in effect a new Patriciate.

German historians often compare the *Zunftekämpfe* of their own country with Italian struggles between *Grandi* and *Popolo*. The comparison, in spite of certain resemblances, is misleading and tends to obscure the essential difference between urban development in Italy and in Germany. The Italian Patriciate was split by schism between a military aristocracy and a capitalist bourgeoisie and the whole communal system of government suffered from the rending shock. In Germany the *Geschlechter* were a small homogeneous body, divided from their subjects only by greater wealth and wider culture. They were not a military class,[1] and were incapable of maintaining a prolonged struggle for power. Their political rivals were men little different from themselves whose ultimate purpose was no more than the substitution of one form of oligarchy for another. Victory of the *Popolo* in Italy meant the immediate triumph of democracy and the beginning of a slow transition to tyranny. When the German Patriciate suffered defeat hostile factions came to terms, party feeling died away and orderly government was soon restored. If necessary, the Emperor intervened to support the conservative party and hasten a peaceful settlement.[2] Conflicts were not sufficiently prolonged nor changes disruptive enough to destroy the habit of corporate action carefully fostered for centuries by guilds and *Burgerstube*. Except among the proletariate, the individual leader, demagogue, Captain of the People or tyrant in embryo did not

---

[1] They were often specifically exempt from military service.
[2] Cf. The intervention of Charles IV in Nuremberg, (1348), of Rupert in Dortmund, (1406), and of Sigismund in the Hansa cities, (1416), and in Constance, (1430).

emerge.[1] In Germany the democratic tendency was strong enough to disturb, but not strong enough to counteract, an oligarchic tradition as powerful as that of Venice.

[1] Zurich provides a solitary exception.   Rudolph Brun, the leader of the attack on the Patriciate, (1339), caused himself to be elected *Burgomeister* for life.   He held office for twenty-one years, (1339–1360), and his tombstone bore the inscription *primus magister civium*.

CHAPTER V

THE RISE OF TYRANNY IN ITALY

INTRODUCTORY. THE RISE OF THE *SIGNORIA* IN ITALY. THE DEVELOPMENT OF THE PRACTICE AND THEORY OF TYRANNY.

1. INTRODUCTORY

THE rise of Tyranny in any community is ultimately due to the victory of the sense of the value of leadership over the sense of the value of individual right. It is easy to form this conclusion from results, but it does not help us to answer certain questions. By what historical process is the surrender of right carried out and why have some communities shown themselves much more ready than others to make such surrenders? A general answer may, perhaps, be found by observing the course of political evolution. In primitive communities the binding force of custom is too strong to permit any considerable delegation of power. When, as in England, custom develops into a common law, administered and amended, at least in part, not only by the consent but with the active co-operation of the people, the sense of individual right is strengthened through constant exercise, and inter-ference with the constitutional organism becomes extremely difficult. Such incorporation of custom and popular control into the constitution is extremely rare. It occurred in England because transition from the static phase of clan organisation was not followed by precocity of political development ; as foreign dangers were not acute and as economic life was simple and lethargic, constitutional evolution was slow and comprehensive. Normally, however, custom gives way to necessity and the special needs of the community compel some surrender of rights in order to secure peace, prosperity and independence. In any society that is at all complicated delegation of function is essential and the smaller and more compact the community the greater will be the sense of security with which transfer of power will be made. In the city state the process was accelerated by the strength of the democratic consciousness ; the citizens were themselves the source of authority and for their own convenience they could transfer that authority to officers of their choice. Partly because the unit of government was small, they failed to see the necessity for retention of control by means of the regular application of constitutional restraints. Competition, greed for wealth and lands, fear of foreign or domestic enemies turned their attention from means to ends and led them to prefer efficiency to direct exercise of rights. In this way authority was delegated first to oligarchs and then to tyrants without any intention of permanent surrender of control. Development along these lines was fairly rapid in the small and highly complicated communities of ancient Greece and medieval Italy ; in the great territorial kingdoms the process was longer, though normally the same end was reached. Gian Galeazzo Visconti, Frederick the Great and Napoleon were alike in basing their power on the accomplishment of great things, which satisfied the ambition and pride of their subjects. The idea of nationality is, in fact, only a halting and less articulate form of the idea of democratic sovereignty underlying civic particularism. The national despotisms of modern Europe slowly came into being for the same reasons of state that called into existence the tyrannies of Greece and Italy. Thus we have the paradox that the

39117

stronger the sense of democratic unity in a free community the greater is the danger of surrender of individual political rights. "Democracy is destroyed by its insatiable craving for the object which it defines to be supremely good." [1]

Investigation of the origin of tyranny in Italy, as an illustration of the general course of political evolution, can be approached from two quite different angles, either by examination of the writings of theorists or by examination of the actual circumstances in which tyranny arose. Both methods have obvious disadvantages. The conclusions of theorists are often vitiated either by indifference to facts or by efforts to force facts into some general system of thought, without adequate consideration of historical development ; the conclusions of historians are liable to error because of the extent of the field to be surveyed and the bewildering number of examples which it is necessary to classify. It is, however, possible to use the two methods to check and correct each other.

It is first of all necessary to glance back at the writings of classical and medieval political thinkers before attempting even a superficial examination of Renaissance theory and practice of tyranny. The resemblance between the constitutional development of Italian cities and that of cities of ancient Greece is close ; in both there were strong oligarchic or aristocratic traditions which early came into conflict with the popular will and in both the victory of the people was the doom of republican freedom. The revival of the study of Aristotle by the Schoolmen and of other classical authors, especially Cicero and Plato, by the Humanists gives the analogy something more than academic interest. In the later middle ages Greek and Roman political theory formed the natural starting-point for investigation of political problems. At the same time Roman law with its absolutist tendencies was, by the Glossators and Post-Glossators, evolved into a system

[1] Plato : *Republic*, 562.

valid for the everyday business of medieval Italy. Add to this the medieval background of political ideas, based on the Bible, the Fathers, the curialist controversialists of the eleventh and twelfth centuries and the Schoolmen, and it becomes plain that to understand what tyranny meant in the Renaissance period without some consideration of the earlier history of the idea is impossible.

Aristotle and Plato both believed that tyranny developed out of democracy, though neither of them undertook a close examination of the way in which tyranny might arise. In the eighth and ninth books of the *Republic* Plato gives a short description of tyranny. " That tyranny is a transformation of democracy is all but obvious. . . . When a tyrant comes into being the root he springs from is the people's champion. . . . And what are the first steps in the transformation of the champion into a tyrant ? . . . Should he find the populace so very compliant that he need make no scruple of shedding kindred blood . . . should he banish and kill and give the signal for cancelling debts and redistributing the land ;—is it not from thenceforth the inevitable destiny of such a man either to be destroyed by his enemies or to become a tyrant, and to be metamorphosed from a man into a wolf ? " Plato's concept of tyranny is mainly ethical and he regards it primarily as the consequence of moral degeneration. When persons dominated by lawless passions become numerous in any community they are " the parents of the Tyrant, who is simply that one of their number whose soul contains the mightiest and hugest tyrant. . . . A city under a tyrant is supremely wicked."

In the *Politics* Aristotle is in agreement with Plato about the democratic origin of tyranny, but he is more concerned with its political than its moral aspects. " A tyranny may grow either out of the most rampant democracy, or out of an oligarchy ; but it is not so likely to arise out of a middle or nearly equal condition." " A tyranny is a compound of oligarchy and democracy in their most extreme forms. . . .   A tyrant is chosen from the people to be their protector against the notables, and in order to prevent them from being injured.   History shows that almost all tyrants have been demagogues, who gained the favour of the people by their accusation of the notables. At any rate it was in this manner that tyrannies arose in the days when cities had increased in power.   Others, which were older, originated in the ambition of kings. . . . Others grew out of the class which were chosen to be chief magistrates. . . .   Others arose out of the customs which oligarchies had of making some individual supreme over the highest offices.   In any of these ways an ambitious man had no difficulty, if he desired, in creating a tyranny. . . ."

Though Roman historians adopted the explanation of the origin of tyranny put forward by Plato and Aristotle and recognised a close connection between demagogues, like the Gracchi, and tyrants, they were not specially interested in this side of the problem.   They emphasised the moral and philosophic rather than the juridical point of view and tended to regard tyranny merely as a degenerate form of monarchy.   This general attitude is clearly illustrated by Seneca : " What is the difference between a tyrant and a king ? . . .   A tyrant differs from a king in deeds, not in name. . . .   Clemency acts as the great distinction between a king and a tyrant. . . .   The one has military force that he may use it as the rampart of peace, the other that he may restrain great hatreds by great fear." [1]   It followed from this concept of tyranny as something hideous and evil, that both Greek and Roman writers praise tyrannicide as an act of patriotism and valour.

The Patristic writers accepted Seneca's definition and continued to regard tyranny as a moral evil.   Gregory

[1] De Clementia, I, 11, 12.

the Great defined the tyrant as " he who does not rule the commonwealth lawfully " and his commentary on the definition shows that he was thinking much less of the positive abuse of power than of the pride and cruelty in the tyrant's soul. Study of the Bible developed the idea that the tyrant's wickedness must be suffered by his subjects, since all government had its origin in the will of God. The doctrine of the divine origin of secular government, implicit in Christ's answer to Pilate : " Thou couldst have no power at all against me except it were given thee from above "—was emphasised by S. Paul in the Epistle to the Romans. " Let every soul be subject unto the higher powers. For there is no power but of God ; the powers that be are ordained of God." Christian submission to every ordinance of man left no place for consideration of questions of legitimacy or justifiable resistance. S. Augustine admitted that even tyrants ruled by God's will and he explicitly condemned tyrannicide. On this Patristic foundation the theory of Divine Right of Kings was subsequently erected.

The strife between the Empire and Papacy in the eleventh and twelfth centuries compelled theocratic apologists to abandon the doctrine of passive submission. Emperors hostile to the Papacy were attacked as tyrants, who used power given them by God in such a way as to endanger the earthly happiness and eternal salvation of their subjects. In the *Policraticus* of John of Salisbury, (written in 1159), we have a direct view of this change of front, represented by means of an elaborate comparison between human society and the human body. The soul, head and body of society are the Church, the prince and the people. The prince is the servant of the Church ; if he behaves as a tyrant, he may lawfully be destroyed. Tyrannicide is defended as, not only lawful, but just and righteous. This teaching is supported by citations from the classics and the Old Testament, but their weight is not quite sufficient to counterbalance the New Testament doctrine of powers ordained by God. The legitimacy or divine origin of tyranny is still admitted ; it is still regarded as a problem belonging to the sphere of morals rather than to that of politics or of law. Scholastic writers for over a century merely elaborated this concept of tyranny, emphasising especially the moral-political element derived from Aristotle. In the *De Regimine Principum* of S. Thomas Aquinas the tyrant is still the wicked ruler who exploits his subjects and governs only for his own interest and pleasure. Marsilius of Padua came nearer to understanding Aristotle's meaning when he tried to determine the difference between tyranny and monarchy by considering the will rather than the well-being of the people, but he does not apply this test in order to distinguish between unlawful seizure of power and the cruel or selfish exercise of the power itself. There was, in fact, a general agreement in the condemnation and abhorrence of tyranny, but it could only be tried by moral tests. The distinction between tyranny and monarchy was purely empirical and was of small value as a protection against new usurpations of power.

2. THE RISE OF THE *Signoria* IN ITALY

Normally, the teaching of the Schoolmen found support in other powerful medieval tendencies. The customary basis of law gave it a sanction that raised it above all personal authority and supplied the necessary juridical counterpart to the doctrine of tyranny as a moral evil. An English legal contemporary of S. Thomas wrote : " The king has as superiors, God and also the law by which he was made king . . . if the king shall be without a bridle, that is, without law, his court shall bridle him." The same idea of the subjection of the ruler to law was present in the feudal contract between overlord and vassals. The oath of allegiance sworn by the subjects of the Kings of Aragon is highly significant : " We, who are as good as you, swear to you, who are no better than we, to accept you as our king and sovereign lord, provided that you observe all our liberties and laws ; but if not, then (we shall) not (accept you)."   In northern and central Italy, by the second half of the thirteenth century, political evolution had passed this stage of development.   The absence of strong monarchy and the decline of feudalism had given local government room to grow at a time when the reception of Roman Law was acting as a solvent of local custom.   Dante compared Italy to a horse, bridled by Justinian (i.e. Roman Law) but grown vicious because no one would ride him.

The dissolution of the bonds of custom was a slow process and merely hastened the normal stages of constitutional evolution.   It is easy to allow objective impressions of incessant movement and recurring fevers of revolution to distract attention from the strong conservative elements in Italian constitutional development and thus to miss the significance of the organic growth of the city state. Italy was no *tabula rasa* for constitution-makers or founders of dynasties. We must reject Burckhardt's famous definition of the Renaissance state as " the outcome of reflection and calculation, the state as a work of art." This conception of the Italian city state is, as Davidsohn, the historian of Florence, has pointed out, " a conception more in keeping with the mode of thought of æsthetics, than with the results of research into historical evolution. A work of art is a creation consciously fashioned, with unity of design, but the political organisation of the communes had arisen out of immediate needs and was adapted by them."

Examination of the history of Italian cities in the later middle ages reveals a strong current running in the direction of despotic government. The process of substituting personal rule for either oligarchic or democratic institutions can first be observed in Lombardy. Ferrara began its surrender to the Estensi about the end of the twelfth century and by 1264 an hereditary *Signoria* had been established. When Bologna accepted Taddeo di Pepoli as its *Signor* in 1337 no city [1] east of the Apennines retained its republican constitution. In central Italy the foundations of tyranny were laid during the residence of the Popes at Avignon, (1305-78). When papal authority was asserted again the expulsion of tyrants from the cities was followed by loss of independence. Tuscany was the last province to succumb to despotic control. The wealth and energy of the *popolo grasso* and a determination to control economic and foreign policy made the Patriciate willing to sacrifice internal peace for the sake of political power. Loss of liberty came through the gradual con- quest of the Arno valley and its hinterland by Florence. When Florence at last accepted the lordship of the Medici in the middle of the fifteenth century nearly all the lesser cities of Tuscany had become part of the Florentine state. Venice remained the only great city which had been able to resist the undermining of its constitution by a tyrant.

The ultimate cause of the rise of tyranny was the strength of the democratic tendency, pulling against the oligarchic constitutions of the communes and leading towards a transfer of power from the people to an arbitrary governor. To understand the provoking cause of this transfer it is necessary to discover why the Patriciate was too weak to resist the democratic tendency ; to explain the process by which the transfer was carried out it is necessary to examine the constitutional stages in the evolution of a *Signoria*. Attention is thus directed to the schism in the Italian Patriciate and to the transformation of the communal constitution.

An entirely different line of investigation has recently been indicated by Mr. P. N. Ure in his *Origin of Tyranny*.

[1] Except Venice.

He believes that "the seventh and sixth century Greek tyrants were the first men in their various cities to realise the political possibilities of new conditions created by the introduction of the new coinage, and that to a large extent they owed their position as tyrants to a financial or commercial supremacy which they had already established before they attained to supreme power in their several states." He develops this view by a comparison with Italian tyranny of the Renaissance. " (The position of the early Greek tyrants) has considerable resemblances to that built up ; . . by the rich bankers and merchants who made themselves despots in so many of the city states of Italy. The most famous of these are the Medici, the family who gave a new power to the currency, by their development of the banking business, and mainly as a result . . . became tyrants of Florence. Santo Bentivoglio of Bologna passed from a wool factory to the throne. Another despot of Bologna was the rich usurer Romeo Pepoli. At Pisa the supreme power was grasped by the Gambacorti with an old merchant named Pietro at their head. At Lodi it was seized by the millionaire Giovanni Vignate. The above instances are taken from Symonds' sixth class of despots of whom he says that ' in most cases great wealth was the original source of despotic ascendancy.' " In Italy, as in Greece, Mr. Ure finds the explanation of the origin of tyranny in the appearance and use of a new form of capital.

Even a perfunctory examination of Mr. Ure's theory will show that it does not provide us with an explanation which meets the facts of Italian history. If the origin of the Italian tyrannies of the Renaissance was the financial revolution caused by the use of a gold currency and bills of exchange, we would expect to find tyrants in those cities where banking, commerce and industry had the greatest development. Exactly the reverse is the case. The first cities to succumb to tyrants were the cities of Lombardy, which, though rich, were never of first class financial importance. Venice never accepted a tyrant. In the cities of Tuscany, especially in Florence and Siena, where banking reached its highest development, the establishment of tyranny was resisted longer than in any other part of Italy. The benevolent despotism of the Medici was not established until a century after the golden age of Florentine banking and commerce.

It cannot, however, be denied that wealth played an important part in the maintenance of tyranny. Money was necessary to hire troops to overawe the city and to relieve the citizens from the burden of military service. It was also necessary for the control of the commercial and industrial interests on which the prosperity of the city was based. It was above all necessary for the preparation of the spectacles and pageants which delighted Italian crowds and, more than anything else, helped to reconcile them to the loss of liberty. It has recently been suggested that the court spectacle satisfied the crowd because it produced by customs, manners, costume and deportment " the illusion of a heroic being, full of dignity and honour, of wisdom and of courtesy." [1] All could not live or represent the ideal life ; it was better that some should so exist than none. " The actions of princes, even daily and common actions, all assume a quasi-symbolic form and tend to raise themselves to the rank of mysteries. Births, marriages and deaths are framed in an apparatus of solemn and sublime formalities. . . . By this sublimating faculty each event became a spectacle for others. . . ." The court and pageants of the tyrant satisfied a craving for a sublimated form of life ; ceremonial and magnificence were an essential part of the apparatus of personal government. Aristotle had long before observed that " by wealth only can the tyrant maintain his guard or his luxury." Wealth was necessary to maintain

[1] Huizinga : *Waning of the Middle Ages.* Chapter 2.

8

tyranny, but it was not, for that reason, a cause of it.

The split in the Patriciate or the schism between the *Grandi* and the *popolo grasso* helps to provide an explanation of the clearly-marked difference between the historical development of Italian cities and those north of the Alps. In the northern cities the Patriciate was composed of a strong mercantile class, united in a policy of commercial exploitation and, in the main, undisturbed by the territorial nobility outside their walls. Similar conditions prevailed in Venice. Throughout the rest of northern and central Italy the Patriciate had no unity of economic or political purpose. The *Grandi* were bent on capturing the governments of the cities which their military prowess had made free ; the *popolo grasso* were equally determined to rule the cities made rich by their industry and foresight. Though almost certainly social in origin, the schism in the Italian Patriciate and the democratic revolt against it were widened and encouraged by political causes. The long struggle between the Empire and the Papacy, fought out on Italian soil, caused the rise of the party groups known as Guelf and Ghibelline.[1] Soon after the death of Frederick II, (1250), the original significance of these party distinctions was forgotten, but the names survived to give a sort of historic sanction to both foreign wars and internal revolution. The Guelf and Ghibelline wars of the later middle ages were due to local factions and to economic jealousies, rather than to any genuine pre-occupation with larger questions of imperial and papal claims. Bartolus of Sassoferato in his tract *De Gelphis et Gebellinis*, (*c.* 1340), states clearly the localisation of party names. " To-day a Guelf might adhere to and support the constitution (*status*) of the party called Ghibelline ; in this he

[1] Davidsohn has shown that the use of *Guelf* and *Ghibelline* as party names was at first localised in Florence and did not extend to other cities until the fourteenth century.

would not be considering either church or Empire, but only particular matters raised in his own city or province. . . . According to the original meaning of the terms . . . a man could not be Guelf in one place and Ghibelline in another. . . . The names are understood to-day in such a way that it is possible for man to be now Guelf and now Ghibelline, since factions are formed about a variety of subjects. For example, a tyrant and his following are called Guelf in one city and to them any good man will be opposed. Within the territory of the city these good men who opposed the tyrant would be called Ghibelline ; if they opposed a tyrant called Ghibelline in another city, they would be called Guelf. . . . Moreover, a man can belong to one faction on one issue and another faction on another. There are, for example, in the city of Perugia many who wish to be deemed Ghibelline in the original meaning of the word, thinking it an honour that long ago their ancestors were Ghibelline nobles. . . . But the same people are Guelf in their support of the constitution which now governs the city. . . . It is decreed by the Pisans that no Guelph should be admitted to public office. . . . This statute ought to be understood to concern only those who may be Guelfs in Pisa. . . . If a Pisan was appointed *rector* of the city of Perugia, whose constitution is Guelf, yet is not hostile but friendly to Pisa, then though the *rector* would be Guelf in Perugia he would not, for this reason be called a Guelf in Pisa, nor would he be disqualified by their statutes."

Bartolus has also some interesting remarks on the legitimacy of party factions. He asks the question : Are factions lawful and is it becoming to an honourable man to belong to them ? " It is plainly illegal and worthy of punishment," he writes, " for a man to belong to a party not for the public good, but for private advantage or that others may be oppressed. . . . The assumption of the names Guelf and Ghibelline is a sign of divisions and factions, but if they are assumed for a just and necessary end, their assumption is lawful. The apostle Paul exclaimed in council, knowing one party were Sadducees and the other Pharisees, ' Men and brethren, I am a Pharisee and the son of a Pharisee.' In Perugia I have known many to join in a conspiracy against tyrants, moved by a just and holy zeal. Because the names imply division and schism, I think that an honest man should not assume one of them except for some great cause, (*nisi ex magna causa*)." Considering the parties from the legal point of view, Bartolus recognises them as *collegia* or corporations. If proved to be irregular and dangerous to the public good, they were illegitimate ; if they were *collegia approbata* or recognised corporations, their internal independence and right to appoint their own officers and legislate for themselves were admitted. In law, partisan corporations were recognised only so far as was consistent with the good of the whole community. " The factions are recognised, but the *bonum publicum* is the limit of their lawfulness."

The treatise of Bartolus shows that it was generally accepted in the fourteenth century that the cities were divided into at least two hostile parties, each of which often had a recognised organisation of its own. The limits he attempted to set to party power had small value, as each party was certain to appear convinced that it was working for the public good and the commune was seldom strong enough to refuse recognition. Thirteenth and fourteenth century statutes of the communes contain numerous prohibitions of the formation and maintenance of parties. In some communes the schism in the Patriciate was widened by explicit proscription or disenfranchisement of the nobles. The Florentine Ordinances of Justice, (1293), and the *Libro Rosso*, (1333), of Perugia alike had as their object the formal exclusion of the *Grandi* from public service, chiefly because of the danger to the merchant oligarchy arising out of co-operation between *Grandi* and *popolo minuto*. Of the result of the Ordinances Villani writes : " Henceforth the artisans and populace had small influence in the commune and the government remained in the grasp of rich and powerful citizens." As a rule, a policy of proscription served only to increase the bitterness of party feeling and to endanger the independence of the commune by providing allies for foreign enemies. It is not therefore surprising that the first *Signori* acquired power as party leaders. The Patriciate, weakened by internal divisions, was unable to resist the popular demand for constitutional change, yet any new phase of constitutional development was bound to be opposed with invincible hatred by the conservative faction. As the prosperity and security of the community could be secured only by strong and stable government, it was inevitable that the party leader, powerful enough to quell his opponents, should sometimes succeed in winning public confidence and be rewarded by a grant of an unlimited dictatorship.

Though the split in the Patriciate and the democratic tendency of the majority in the communes normally led to the overthrow of oligarchic government, it did not follow that the *Signor* as tyrant sprang fully armed from the consequent anarchy. Stories of chroniclers and Ferrari's famous computation of three hundred massacres and seven thousand revolutions between A.D. 1000 and 1500 have tended to give the impression that Italian constitution-making was always carried out in a hurry as the result of tumults in the Piazza. Though the number of revolutions cannot be denied they often had no more constitutional significance than a modern general election ; they were, in fact, the natural means of expressing the popular will in communities which had failed to evolve a system of democratic representation. In the thirteenth and fourteenth centuries Italian politicians showed themselves as practical as they were passionate, as conservative of form as they were violent in method. Usually they did not attempt to interfere with the structure of the constitution, but continually modified it by the creation of new offices. Preservation of obsolete machinery and multiplication of checks on the free action of communal officials helped to produce constitutions too elaborate and slow moving to be organs of strong government. To correct this defect the practice grew up of delegating authority to a few officials, who in times of crises were entrusted with absolute power. Scope was thus given for the ambition and energy of individuals, who, with the support of one section of the Patriciate and the discontented *Popolo*, were able gradually to manipulate the communal constitution in such a way as to lay the foundations of an hereditary principate. The process can best be illustrated by observation of the historical development of the offices of Podesta of the Commune, Podesta of Merchants, Captain of the People and War Captain. The change from the rule of the Patriciate to the rule of a tyrant was not a cataclysm ; it was a slow transition on an inclined plane.

By the end of the twelfth century modification of the communal constitution by party pressure had already begun. The tendency to concentrate powers in the hands of a single official was shown in the rise of a new executive officer, the Podesta, who at first acted in co-operation with the Consuls and then replaced them altogether. His functions were carefully defined in the oldest statutes of the communes. He was the military leader, the chief executive officer and the first judge of the commune, but he was bound by his oath to adminster the law, as defined by custom and statute, and to consult the Councils of the citizens on all important business. All legislation was in the hands of the Council ; the Podesta could not repeal or alter a single statute. His most difficult duties were the defence or subjection of the *contado* and the prevention of open war between factions. At the end of his term of office his accounts and general policy were reviewed by a

special commission (*sindacato*) appointed for the purpose.
All parties watched him jealously, lest he should favour
one of them unduly. In consequence even his private life
was hedged about by petty restrictions. In Florence, for
example, he was never allowed to interview anyone alone,
to talk often with the same citizen, to go out to dinner
or supper parties, or indeed to go out at all unless accompanied by gentlemen of his household. His position was
in many ways like that of a constitutional king ; he was
the formal representative of the state, fully subject to the
will of the Council and to the laws of the commune.

Development of the office of Podesta in the direction
of tyranny reveals itself through the increase of the
Podesta's authority and the extension of his term of office.
Increase of authority occurred in times of foreign or
domestic crisis, when *arbitrium* or absolute power was
bestowed upon him. In times of war he was sometimes
granted full military control ; in times of domestic strife
he was given a discretionary power of punishment which
released him from the bondage of the law. In 1242, for
example, the Council of Reggio granted the Podesta
liberty to do whatsoever he wished (*libertatem faciendi
quicquid vellet*) in order that peace might be secured ; in
Bologna, (1252), he was granted *Liberum arbitrium* in the
punishment of murder ; in Como, (1259), *arbitrium* in the
punishment of all crimes and acts of violence committed
in the city or district. The significance of these grants
of discretionary power lay in the fact that they released
the Podesta from his bondage to the law. First he was
granted dispensations for particular cases, then he was
given authority to suspend the law altogether. The need
for strong government forced the communes to bestow
more power on the Podesta than was permitted by their
statutes. The Councils suspended their control before
they abdicated.

Side by side with the development of the arbitrary

power of the Podesta was the extension of his term of office. Originally he was appointed for one year and, though many statutes forbade the frequent election of the same person, the demand for a stable government was often stronger than fear of an individual. Not only was the same person re-elected again and again, but the term of his office was extended by degrees from one year to three, five or ten years. Finally a Podesta was appointed for life. This prolongation of the term of office was closely connected with the strife of parties. The Podesta, as party leader, was kept in office in order that he might advance the interest of his faction and repress its enemies. The process can be illustrated from the history of Ravenna and Ferrara. In the second half of the thirteenth century the Podesta in Ravenna was a party leader, owing his perenniality in the first place to the war between the factions led by the rival families of Polenta and Traversari. After the expulsion of the Traversari from the city, (1275), Guido di Polenta became Podesta from 1286 to 1294 and his son, Lamberto, was Podesta between 1298 and 1310 and again in 1313 and 1314. Lamberto died childless in 1316 and his nephew, Guido Novello, succeeded him as Podesta. In 1322 Ostasio, cousin of Guido, was Podesta and Captain of the People. It is not certain at what time the office of Podesta began to be held for life by a member of the Polenta family, but it was at least as early as the rule of Ostasio in the third decade of the fourteenth century. During Ostasio's lifetime his son, Bernadino, was elected Podesta as a sign that the office had become hereditary. Bernadino's sons used the title " lords and rulers of the city of Ravenna," (1390). In this way the *Signoria* of the Polenta developed directly from the transformation of the office of Podesta into a permanent and hereditary dignity.

In Ferrara the process was earlier and much more rapid. It is often stated that the Margraves of Este (in the Euganean hills, near Arqua), became lords of Ferrara as

early as 1208, thus anticipating later *Signoria* by half a
century.   The evidence on which the statement rests has
recently been discredited and it is now possible to bring
the history of Ferrara into line with that of other cities.
Ferrara, important because of its strategic position in the
lower basin of the Po, lay just within the borders of the
Papal States and was deeply involved in the Guelf and
Ghibelline contest.   Rivalry between factions, led by the
Estensi (Guelf) and Salinguerra (Ghibelline), can be traced
back to the last decade of the twelfth century.   Salinguerra was Podesta of the commune in 1195, 1199, 1203
and 1207 ; Azzo VI d'Este [1] in 1196 and 1205, his son
Aldrovandino, in 1212 and 1213.   In 1213 a treaty was
made between the factions in which it was agreed that the
exiled party of Salinguerra should return to the city and
that in future Aldrovandino and Salinguerra should
nominate the Podesta jointly or, if they differed, entrust
the appointment to two arbitrators.   The agreement shows
the suspension of the right of the commune to elect the
Podesta.   Aldrovandino died in 1215 and, as his brother
Azzo was a mere child, the party of Salinguerra ruled
Ferrara for twenty-five years. Salinguerra exercised
absolute power over the city, supported by the *Popolo*
because his rule brought peace and prosperity.   He does
not appear to have used the title of Podesta and there is
no record of a formal transfer of authority to him by the

[1] Azzo VI.   Margrave d'Este, 1212.

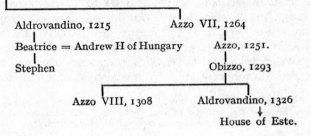

Aldrovandino, 1215   Azzo VII, 1264

Beatrice = Andrew II of Hungary   Azzo, 1251.

Stephen   Obizzo, 1293

Azzo VIII, 1308   Aldrovandino, 1326

House of Este.

commune. In 1340 his government was overthrown by a combination of Venetians, jealous of the city's prosperity, with a Guelf army led by Azzo d'Este. Azzo was Podesta of Ferrara in 1242, 1244, 1247 to 1251 and 1258. We do not know whether after 1251 he was elected for a term of years or for life. He never used any other title than that of Podesta and during the last years of his rule the office was held by others. There can be no doubt that he was lord of Ferrara until his death in 1264, and it is probable that the only constitutional indication of his position as *Signor* lay in the delegation of the office of Podesta to his own nominee. Just before or immediately after Azzo's death his grandson Obizzo, though still a minor, was elected by the Podesta, Council and popular assembly of Ferrara as " governor, rector, general and perpetual lord of the city and district of Ferrara." In the electoral decree Obizzo was designated *nepos et heres* of Azzo VII and the power bestowed on him was " *iurisdictionem et potestatem atque imperium intus et extra ipsius civitatis.*" We can see at the same time the hereditary principle emerging and the influence of the civilian idea of *imperium* transferred to the *Signor* by the people.[1] Thus, in Ferrara by 1264 an hereditary *Signoria* was established, having its origin in the office of Podesta, which was captured by the military leader of the Guelf party in the city.

A similar process was going on in all communes where strong government was equally necessary. For example, Boso di Doaria was elected Podesta of Cremona for ten years, (1248), and Podesta for life of Sonzino, (1255), and of San Giorgio d'Orsi, (1259). In Tuscany Charles I of Anjou was chosen as Podesta of many cities ; Florence, Lucca, Pistoia, Prato and other communes accepted him as Podesta for six years. He was also Senator [2] of Rome

---

[1] Obizzo's election may have been carried out with special formality because he was not only a minor, but illegitimate.
[2] The Senator was the Roman equivalent of the Podesta.

for life and "lord and perpetual governor" of the cities of Brescia and Alessandria. He exercised his functions by deputy and, in addition to his control of Tuscan cities, eight Lombard communes submitted to his vicars. Charles obviously recognised the value of the office of Podesta as a means of securing political control.

In the second half of the thirteenth century the dangerous potentialities of the Podesta were recognised by many cities, especially after the sharpest phase of the Guelf and Ghibelline conflict had ended with the death of Conradin, (1268). Numerous statutes illustrate the attempt to keep him in subjection to the commune. Statutes of Bologna and Vicenza, (1250), prohibited the re-election of a Podesta who had served within three years of the date of election ; Padua (1277) decreed the death penalty as punishment for the proposal that the Podesta should be re-elected for a second year. Other statutes provided that he should not be elected *ad vocem* or *ad clamorem*, showing fear of the tumultuous choice of the popular assembly. In Bologna the electors were shut up in conclave in order that the outgoing Podesta might not influence their decision. In the closing years of the century a number of cities cut down the Podesta's term of office to six months. Stringent laws were passed against the dispensation of the *Sindacato* and against the bestowal of *arbitrium* even for a limited purpose or term. The Councils sought to retain or recover the control of all important business. In many cities the *Anziani*, Priors or Cabinet of Elders diverted power from the Podesta to themselves. Their appearance was a sign of the discontent of the *Popolo* with communal government, a discontent which found an even more powerful representative in the Captain of the People. The rise of new popular institutions combined with legislative prohibitions to block the evolution of the Podesta into the *Signor*. He was, in fact, too much the official of the Patriciate to be acceptable as

Signor in strongly democratic communities. It is not an accident that of the five great signorial families of north Italy, (Carrara, Este, Gonzaga, Scala and Visconti), only one and that the oldest, the house of Este, traced the origin of its power to the office of Podesta.

A much more important factor in the growth of the *Signoria* was the democratisation of the communal constitution by the development of the offices of Podesta of Merchants and Captain of the People. The Podesta of Merchants represented the commercial and financial interests of the guilds, often united in a *societas populi*. He owed his power primarily to control of the military organisations of the guilds and to the support of special executive and judicial institutions. The way in which the captainship developed out of this office can be illustrated from the history of Parma. Representatives of the guilds began to confer with the council of Parma as early as 1226 : in 1231 a definite prohibition of their co-operation in legislation suggests resistance to a claim to political power. A rising of the guilds and *Popolo* against the Patriciate broke out in 1244 and the Podesta of Merchants was proclaimed Captain of the People. After a struggle, the right to share in the elections of officers of the commune was granted to the " Consuls of the wards and guilds." By this means the *Popolo* of Parma not only acquired a share in the government, but promoted their leader to be one of the chief executive officers of the commune. The example of Parma was followed by other cities. Florence, Piacenza and Perugia appointed Captains of the People in 1250 and within thirty years all the communes where the democratic tendency was strong took advantage of the Guelf and Ghibelline wars to secure the protection of this new official. The Captain had his own guard, courts of justice and revenue. He lived in the palace of the commune and was advised by councils from which the *grandi* were usually excluded. Ambitious *grandi* began to seek election and, with the victory of the democratic movement, the office came to be the foundation of absolute hereditary power.

As with the office of Podesta, the development of the Captainship can be observed through the increase of authority and the extension of the term of office. Some historians have considered that the Captain of the People was primarily a military officer and that he was appointed to limit the power of the Podesta by taking over his military duties. They seek to explain his increase of authority as the usurpation of a military dictator. Salzer has shown that this explanation is incorrect.[1] The Captain of the People was before everything else the leader of the political organisation of the *Popolo*. When the *Popolo* secured control over the communal constitution their leader inevitably became the chief officer of the city ; he bore the title of " Captain of the commune and of the people " ; in the popular interest he claimed the right of control over the Executive and the administration of justice. It is not necessary to delay over the increase of his authority, as it followed the lines already indicated in the case of the Podesta. The same tendency to grant *arbitrium* or discretionary powers reappears for the same purpose and with the same results.

Extension of term of office also developed along lines parallel to the extension of the term of the Podesta. The process can be illustrated from the history of Milan and Verona. In Milan a triple system of government had been established at the end of the twelfth century, by means of which political power had been divided unequally between the party of the consuls, (higher nobility), the party of the *Molta*, (majority : lesser nobility and *popolo grasso*), and the party of S. Ambrose, (mainly the craft guilds). As the parties appear to have been fairly evenly

[1] Ernst Salzer : Ueber die Anfänge der Signorie in Oberitalien, Cap. i, § 3.

balanced, strife between factions was incessant and a career
was open to the talents of the able party leader.   The
office of Podesta of the People,[1] representing the party of
S. Ambrose, appeared in 1225.   The date of its transformation into the captainship cannot be fixed, though Martino
della Torre, leader of the *Popolo*, exercised all its main
functions between 1259 and 1263, while holding office as
Podesta of the People.   After the death of Martino his
brother Philip succeeded him as Podesta of the People
and was elected " perpetual lord of the people of Milan,"
(1263–5) ;   Philip was succeeded by his nephew, Napo,
who was also elected for life.   Resistance to the domination
of Milan by the Torriani family was organised by the
Archbishop, Ottone Visconti,[2] leader of the *grandi*.   In
1277 he defeated the Torriani in open battle and from
that time until his death in 1295 he ruled Milan.   It is not
certain whether he based his authority on an election by
the citizens in 1277, or on a re-election in 1282, or on his
ecclesiastical dignity.   He never seems to have used the
title of " lord of Milan," but his intention to found an
hereditary *Signoria* was never in doubt.   In 1287 he prepared the way for a successor by causing the election of his
great-nephew, Matteo, as Captain of the People for one
year ;   the appointment was renewed for a further year
in 1288 and in 1289 and 1294 the term was fixed at five
years.   When Archbishop Ottone died in 1295 Matteo

---

[1] Another term for Podesta of Merchants.

[2] Ottone Visconti,
Archbishop of Milan, † 1295

Obizzo
|
Tebaldo
|
Matteo, † 1322

Galeazzo, † 1328, *Luchino*, † 1349   Giovanni,   Stefano, 1327.
                                          Archbishop, † 1349.
Azzo, † 1339
                                          House of Visconti.

inherited his authority, but still used only the style of Captain of the People. In 1299 he was again elected for five years and in 1301 his son, Galeazzo, was elected for one year. These elections for a fixed term show that at the end of the thirteenth century the Visconti had not yet gained the full confidence of the Milanese. For reasons which are obscure, Matteo and his son went into voluntary exile in 1302 and the Torriani once more became the chief family in the city. Guido Torre was chosen Captain of the People for one year in 1307 and in the following year he was elected for life. Matteo seized the opportunity of the expedition of Henry VII to return to Milan. Henry granted him the imperial vicariate in 1311 and his election as Captain of the People probably followed immediately. When Matteo turned Guelf and dropped the imperial title, (1317), he was elected by the council of the city *dominus generalis* of Milan. Though the hereditary right of the family to the Signoria was not ever in doubt after 1317, a positive statement that the succession should follow the direct, legitimate, male line of Matteo Visconti does not appear until the appointment of Archbishop Giovanni as Vicar of Milan in 1349. More than thirty years earlier the hereditary *Signoria* of the Visconti had existed in fact.

A similar process can be more briefly traced in Verona. After the fall of Ezzelino di Romana, (1259), a popular revolution broke out in the city, as a result of which Mastino della Scala, leader of the *Popolo*, was elected Podesta of Merchants in 1260-1. In 1270 his brother, Alberto, was appointed to the same office, probably for life. The office of Captain of the People cannot be traced before 1269, when Mastino was appointed for one year ; from that time until his death in 1277 his election was renewed annually. Mastino seems to have made no open attempt to nominate a successor, beyond securing his brother's election as Podesta of Merchants. After his death a great *concio* or mass meeting of citizens was held and the Podesta asked if it were the will of the people that Alberto della Scala [1] should be appointed captain of the people for life. The councils, guilds and nobles voted separately and unanimously in his favour and the people acclaimed him tumultuously as their lord. He assumed the title of "Captain and rector of the officials of the guilds and of all the people of Verona." This election was the origin of the *Signoria* of the Scaligeri at Verona. Alberto caused his son, Bartolomeo, to be appointed co-rector during his lifetime, thus preparing the way for the peaceful succession of 1301. Bartolomeo was elected Captain for life in 1301 and his successor, Alboino, was elected first Captain and then, three days later, Podesta of Merchants for life. In 1329 Alberto and Mastino II, were appointed captains of the city and districts of Verona on the express grounds that it had been the wish and intention of Cangrande that his nephews should succeed him and in 1359 the hereditary title was explicitly recognised in the election of Cansignorio and Paolo Alboino. They were accepted as *domini generales* of the city because they were sons of Mastino II and the rights of their heirs for ever were admitted. Out of the offices of Podesta of Merchants and Captain of the People the hereditary Signoria of the Scaligeri had developed.

The War Captainship was an office entirely distinct from that of the Captain of the People, though sometimes they were held by the same person. As we have seen, the Captain of the People was primarily the political leader of the *Popolo*; the War Captain was a commander-

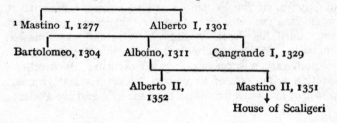

[1] Mastino I, 1277   Alberto I, 1301

Bartolomeo, 1304   Alboino, 1311   Cangrande I, 1329

Alberto II, 1352   Mastino II, 1351

House of Scaligeri

in-chief appointed to take over the military duties of the Podesta of the Commune. His first recorded appearance was in 1233–4 when, in the communal palace of Parma, Azzo d'Este was solemnly invested with the banner of the city and entrusted with the supreme command of the army. Over twenty years later (1259) Uberto Palavicini became Captain General of Milan and exercised the powers of a military dictator over the city until 1264. The office seldom became a permanent part of the communal constitution, though it was used at times of special danger from foreign enemies. The relations of the house of Anjou to Florence and other Tuscan cities at the end of the thirteenth and the beginning of the fourteenth centuries had their origin in military necessity. It was as War Captain of the Guelf party that Robert of Naples was granted the lordship of Florence for five years, (1313). In the same way, when the Pisan war was going against them, the Florentines invited the Duke of Athens to act as Captain General of their armies, (1341). In north-west Italy William of Montferrat used the office of War Captain to weld together a number of cities under his rule, (1260–92). His position differed from that of other *Signori* because it rested, in part, on a feudal basis. The communes submitted to him on terms and his powers of taxation and alienation were limited by bargains closely resembling feudal contracts. The lordship of the house of Montferrat must be regarded as exceptional. The War Captainship, as a rule, was used only as a temporary expedient and lacked the connection with political organisation necessary to its development in democratic communities.

When Lucchino Visconti accepted the lordship of Alessandria (1347) he wrote to the citizens " we love peace, hate discord and intend to maintain our subjects and territories in a state of peace and tranquillity, and for no other reason than the maintenance of peace do we wish

9

to interfere in the affairs of Alessandria." These words provide a summary explanation of the transformation of the communes into *Signorie*. The democratic tendency, party strife, foreign war and the success of experiments in personal government had combined to discredit the older republican forms. A clause in the statutes of Cremona was characteristic of the general shifting of confidence from institutions to individuals. " To be without a prince is impossible ; cities and all else without a prince are in confusion."

3. THE DEVELOPMENT OF THE PRACTICE AND THEORY OF TYRANNY

Through the development of the personal authority of communal officials and the extension of their term of office, the republican constitution, often retaining its ancient form, was slowly transformed into a *Signoria* or principate. The signs of independence characteristic of the communes had been the free election of its officers, especially the Podesta and Captain, and the exercise of executive and legislative power by councils of citizens. With the foundation of the *Signoria* these prerogatives began to disappear, either partially or altogether. The Podesta no longer held office for six months or a year, but at the pleasure of the Signor to whom he owed unconditional obedience. In Padua, for example, Jacopo di Carrara was granted at the time of his election as *Signor*, (1318), the power of nominating the Podesta and determining his salary and household arrangements. During the rule of the Caminesi as Signori of Treviso (1283–1312) the following statute regulated the choice of Podesta : " Every Podesta or Rector who shall come to govern the city of Treviso, together with his judges, soldiers and all his household, shall and ought to be of the Guelf Party and of the party and fellowship of the noble man, Lord G. da Camino, Captain General of the city and district of

Treviso. If any one does not so wish, or offers opposition of any sort . . . his head shall be cut off . . . and all his goods shall be forfeit for ever to the Commune of Treviso."

Full financial control was usually granted to the *Signor*, who gradually acquired command of all the resources of the City. Thus, in 1293, Reggio granted to Azzo d'Este an unconditional power over the persons, goods and property of the commune and of each individual citizen (" *omnia et singula facere de personis et rebus et bonis communis, civitatis, universitatis et singularum personarum civitatis R . . .* "). The decrees of the *Signor* could always override the statutes of the commune, even when published only in his own name. The councils were dependent on his pleasure, as he had exclusive right of summons and dissolution and was not bound by their decisions. The number of their members declined and the right of free election was replaced by Signorial nomination. At the same time the political activities of the guilds and their councils were suppressed. When Guido Bonacolsi was appointed Captain of the People in Mantua, (1299), he was granted power " to rule and govern the city, district and commune of Mantua at his own mere, pure, free and general will and pleasure, (*arbitrium et voluntatem*), without council or with council, as it shall seem to him good and useful." The *Signor*, in fact, exercised a discretionary or absolute power over every department of state.

Although the citizens seemed to have abdicated in favour of the *Signor*, they probably did not at first contemplate a permanent surrender of control. They regarded the *Signor* as their representative and believed that they could always depose him, if they were satisfied that he was not acting in their interests. By express decree of the people he had received *arbitrium* or release from the bondage of law. He was a tyrant only if power had not been lawfully transferred to him, or if his acts after such a transfer were harmful to his subjects. Tyranny consisted, not in the exercise of arbitrary power, legally bestowed, but in failure to use it for the purpose for which it had been transferred. The *Signoria* was a constitutional form of government because its legal basis was an act of popular sovereignty, the free, independent and deliberate election of the *Signor* by the citizens.

That these considerations were not merely academic, but had positive judicial significance can be proved from the legal archives of the *Signoria*. For our purposes it is worth while to examine two lawsuits of the fourteenth century, one from Treviso and the other from Padua.[1] In Treviso, two years after the downfall of the despotic government of the Caminesi and the restoration of a republican form of Government, (1314), the commune challenged the right of the Avogari family to collect certain tolls at the city gates. The commune was able to show that the tolls had always belonged to the commune until the Caminesi had bestowed them on the Avogari family. The trial turned on the validity of this grant, that is, on whether the Caminesi, as *Signori* of Treviso, had the right to make it. The commune disputed, not the validity of the particular grant, but the general legitimacy of the Caminesi government, which, it was maintained, was tyrannical and therefore incapable of actions valid in law.[2] A number of witnesses, most of whom were old and influential citizens, were summoned by the commune to

[1] Cited by Professor Francisco Ercole in his edition of Salutati's *Tractatus de Tyranno*, pp. 68–76. The documents for the Trevisan suit are printed by G. B. Picotti in *I Caminesi e la lora signoria in Treviso*, pp. 303–15.

[2] The Caminesi *Signori*:

Gherado da Camino b. 1240, *c.* 1306
Captain General of Treviso, 1283–1306.

Rizzardo b. 1274 ?, 1312.
Captain of Treviso, 1303–6, jointly with Gherado; alone, 1306–12.

Gueccellone, 1324
Captain of Treviso, 12 April–14th Dec., 1312.

answer in court a series of questions relating to the alleged tyranny of the Caminesi. The questions dealt with (1) the circumstances and form of elections to the Captainship; (2) the office of Captain and (3) the tyrannical acts of the Caminesi as Captains. In answer to the first question witnesses described how before 1283 Treviso had been divided by factions, the White or Guelf party of the Caminesi and the Red or Ghibelline party of the Castelli; how in 1283 the Reds were driven from the city; how Gherado da Camino was elected for life Captain General of the city and district of Treviso by " the councils of the Courts and the Council of Three Hundred "; and how he was unanimously accepted by about two thousand citizens in the *Concio* on the same day, before breakfast, taking the oath of Captain and receiving oaths of obedience in the communal palace. A notarial instrument transferring authority to him was drafted and was afterwards bound up in the communal statute book. The election of Gherado's son, Rizzardo, was admitted by several witnesses to have taken place in the lifetime of his father. One witness, a judge, stated that he had read the charter drafted for Rizzardo's election and had kept it in his house for many months until it was borrowed from him and not returned. It was admitted that at their elections the Caminesi were given arbitrary power over Treviso. The second question —the nature of the office of Captain—elicited some interesting answers from witnesses. Friar Petrus de Arpo said that, according to the intention of Trevisans, to be captain meant to have power to act for, work for and administer the affairs of the city and district of Trevisa as the holder should please, (*quod esse capitaneus . . . est esse dominus in agendo et faciendo et administrando civitatem Tervisii et districtum ad suam voluntatem*). Montorius de Villanova defined the Captain as " lord of cities and districts." He further stated that a Captain imposed his will on his subjects, either by his own action or through his officials, adding

" to act thus is not to discharge public duties well nor in a manner worthy of respect." Manfred, a tailor, stated that he had seen Gherado exercising his office of Captain by pardoning malefactors and murderers and again and again condemning the innocent. The intention of the Trevisans was that the Captain should use and exercise arbitrary power over the city and districts ; the office was harmful to public welfare and an evil dignity. Rolandinus, the judge, made a fuller statement : " To-day the functions and powers of the Captainship are interpreted at the good pleasure of Captains and, if they please, they can use it as an euphemism for the name of tyranny (*paliare volencium nomen tyranie*). . . . The office and dignity of the Captainship are good, according to the true meaning of the office, because government is good, but as a cloak for tyrannical depravity, they are evil, because it is evil to destroy and waste subjects and their goods." These answers show that Trevisans had begun to criticise their own constitutional machinery and to perceive the danger of bestowal of arbitrary power. The Captain was not necessarily a tyrant, but it was easy for him to become one. Replying to the third question, witnesses cited various examples of tyrannical acts of the Caminesi. Friar Petrus de Arpo said that " when one man killed another and was banished for homicide, Gherado pardoned him by his arbitrary will, and when another was condemned to death, he pardoned him arbitrarily ; he also caused to be condemned persons not condemned by law or statute, giving and cancelling sentences as he pleased. . . ." The judge Rolandinus stated that he had seen Gherado appointing whom he pleased as magistrates and doing all things in the city contrary to the will and knowledge of the Council of Three Hundred, though sometimes he caused the Council bell to be rung and, summoning country people and others who were not councillors, he caused such statutes as he pleased to be passed, as if in council. Benvenuto de Castegnedo gave evidence that "he had seen and heard Gherado daily issuing commands to all men in the City . . . to 'do thus' and 'do thus' and they obeyed him; he led the men of Treviso on a military expedition to Friuli and to any other place he wished: he imposed and caused to be imposed on them taxes and tasks according to his pleasure, destroying the goods and possessions of the commune . . . and making gifts by special favour to one and another, as he pleased from the goods and possessions of the commune. . . ." All these witnesses agree that Rizzardo's rule was worse and more tyrannical than that of his father. It was determined on the evidence that the Caminesi had been tyrants and, consequently, the Avogari lost their case.

The finding of the Trevisan court was based, not on the illegitimate origin of the Signoria, but on the way in which government had been exercised. The witnesses had explicitly and in detail admitted that the *Signoria* of the Caminesi had a legal basis in the free and independent choice of the citizens. No witness for the commune denied the right of the Caminesi to arbitary power, but all were agreed that they had abused this right by overriding the law, reversing judicial sentences and wasting the substance of the commune and its citizens. Their evidence shows a positive recognition for juridical purposes of two kinds of tyranny; the tyrant *ex defectu tituli*, who had illegally usurped power, and the tyrant *ex parte exercitii*, whose government was unjust. The phraseology comes from the *De Tyranno* of Bartolus, (*c.* 1340), but, as we have seen, the distinction was put to practical use by the Trevisans in 1314–15. Over sixty years later the citizens of Padua made use of the same distinction in reversing certain decrees of the last years of the government of Francesco Carrara after it had been overthrown by Gian Galeazzo Visconti, (1388). The decrees were declared by witnesses to be illegal, not because of the illegitimacy of the govern-

ment, but because of the injustice of the decrees themselves and of the motives behind them.[1] The witnesses
were agreed that they were bound to acknowledge the
legitimacy of the Carraresi government since they had
in their archives, not only the civic statute or solemn popular
decree which had transferred to one of the Carraresi
unlimited and arbitrary power over the city, but also an
imperial diploma sanctioning the exercise of that power.
These examples, which could be paralleled by others from
northern and central Italy, show that the legal stability
of the *Signoria* was secured by the free consent of the
people and the sanction of the Emperor, and that it continued to be legitimate for just so long as power was
exercised for the purpose for which it had been bestowed.

It is easy for us to see that abuse of power was a necessary
consequence of the bestowal of *arbitrium* and that the
popular origin of government would in course of time be
forgotten. These considerations were not obvious to
subjects, conscious of their sovereign powers and unable
to realise that political faculties atrophy from want of
use. The *Signori* took full advantage of the decline in the
political interests and aptitudes of their subjects. They
had already for their own ends perverted the democratic
tendency; they now sought to crush it out of existence by

[1] *Vide* Roberto Cessi: Il Malgoverno di Francesco il Vecchio,
signore di Padova, (Venezia 1907). A number of witnesses gave
evidence against the government of Francesco, stating that he continually issued arbitrary commands and harassed his subjects by
forced loans, free gifts and interference with their testamentary
dispositions. One witness said : " tanquam homo, qui fuit officiallis
dicti domini Francisci . . . ivit ad certas personas dicendo sibi ex
parte dicti domini Francisci . . . quod deberent condere testa-
mento et dicendo eis : Dominus noster Franciscus de Carraria vult
quod faciatis testamentum et vult quod faciatis sic et sic." Another
witness said : " quod et quando dominus Franciscus . . . equitabat
per civitatem Padue ser Franciscum Vifarellum se ascondere, si
comode poterat, dicendo : iste diabollus numquam morietur et si
posem facere, ego vellem potius quod omnes meretrices haberent
mea bona, quam iste diabollus infernalis, et si ego posem ipsa in mari
proicerem vel igne comburem."

superimposing on it other claims to the enjoyment of power. The chief means by which this policy was carried out were the development of the hereditary principle and the recognition of the *Signoria* by the Pope and the Emperor, as lords paramount.

The popular basis of the *Signor's* power was shown in his election, which immediately followed the death of the reigning prince. The election was carried out by the Council of the commune and ratified by the assent of the *concio* or mass meeting of citizens. Sometimes electoral proceedings were initiated by the smaller council of guilds or elders. After his election the *Signor* was formally invested with a sceptre and the banner and keys of the city, as symbols of authority. It was inevitable that the election should become more and more a matter of form as the office of *Signor* became hereditary in one family. The hereditary principle was secured, partly by the practice of *condominium* or joint rule of the *Signor* and his heir and partly by causing the heir's right of succession to be recognised during the *Signor's* lifetime. We have already seen how the hereditary principle was established by the Visconti in Milan and the Carraresi in Verona. In Ferrara a statute of 1292 explicitly recognised the right of the *Signor* to designate his successor. At the election of Loysius Gonzaga as Captain of Mantua in 1328 he was granted power to delegate authority in his lifetime as well as to nominate his successor. The practice of *condominium* and the *Signor's* power of designation complicated the succession and retarded the development of primogeniture. The exclusion of illegitimate sons from the succession, as in Milan, 1349, was a sign of the substitution of the hereditary principle for popular election. Popular political control, exercised perhaps only once in a generation and then along lines pre-ordained for it, became little more than a legal fiction.

The chief means used, not only to establish hereditary

succession but to escape from the servitude of popular control, was an increasing emphasis on rights bestowed on the *Signor* by the Pope or Emperor in the form of a Vicariate. The technical legal superiority of these overlords, once fiercely resented, was first invoked to give an additional sanction to the foundation of a dynasty and then indicated as the true and ultimate source of authority. It must be remembered that few Italian cities enjoyed *merum imperium* or sovereignty in the full sense of the term. Venice, Naples, and the islands that lay outside the old kingdom of Italy perhaps possessed it, but the rest of the peninsula was technically either *terra ecclesiae* or *terra imperii*. As lawyers admitted that papal or imperial ratification was necessary to create an absolutely competent and legal government, the *Signori* were careful to secure the sanction of their superiors as soon as possible. Formal ratification of the constitutional change from republic to *Signoria* was often followed by the grant of a Vicariate [1] or delegation of the rights of the overlord to the Signor. The authority of the superior was seldom made a pretext for active interference and it was therefore natural that more and more stress should be laid on its positive creative power. Imperial and papal Vicars represented themselves as *Signori*, established and confirmed in their absolute and hereditary rights by diplomas and decrees which no popular verdict could annul. They used every means in their power to secure their dynastic and territorial interests by obtaining recognition as Princes of the Church or of the Empire. Thus, by diploma of the Emperor Wenceslas, Milan became a duchy in 1394-5 and the succession was secured to the house of Visconti. In 1432 Sigismund bestowed on Francesco Gonzaga the title of Marquis; in 1452 Frederick III created Borso d'Este

---

[1] These Vicariates were usually granted at first to individuals, but when such individuals succeeded in founding *Signorie* the vicariates almost invariably were transformed into hereditary dignities.

Duke of Modena and Reggio : in 1470 a papal decree transformed the Vicariate of Ferrara into a duchy with Borso as its duke.   Bestowal of such dignities was always accompanied by an explicit recognition of hereditary succession according to the rules of primogeniture.   The duchies and marquisates of modern Italy, with dynastic rights and policies as clearly defined as those of older transalpine monarchies, were the outcome of the creation of papal and imperial superiors.   The *Signor* of the city, representing the free choice of the citizens, had become the hereditary territorial prince.

During the period in which the *Signoria* was growing up and while the *Signor* was laying the foundations of absolute hereditary power, the theory of tyranny was passing through important phases of development.   Its history shows the strength and variety of Italian political influences and also a persistent search for a formula to explain and justify contemporary forms of government. At the end of the thirteenth and the beginning of the fourteenth century the failure of the theocratic policy of the Papacy, the extraordinarily vigorous development of the city state and the classical studies of the first humanists combined to bring about a reaction from the predominantly ethical concept of tyranny hitherto accepted.   The identification of the tyrant with the wicked prince persisted, but the wicked prince was sharply contrasted with the wise governors of a republic.   Tyranny and freedom were set against each other as the natural products of monarchical and republican government.   Dante described Ceseno at the foot of the Apennines as " lying between the plain and the mount as it lives between tyranny and freedom." [1]   In the sermons of S. Bernadino of Siena the tyrant was the *rector rapti* or plundering governor who threatened and exploited his subjects.   Cola di Rienzo,

---

[1] *Inferno. XXVII,* 54.   Malatesta of Rimini became *Signor* of Cesena in 1314.

Petrarch and Boccaccio use the word *tyrant* as a synonym for violence and pride and it was generally admitted that these vices were an inevitable characteristic of rulers who had overthrown republican constitutions. Tyranny was, in fact, the necessary consequence of autocracy.

This formula ceased to be adequate when politicians and theorists recognised that there could be, not only more than one form of constitutional government, but also more than one form of tyranny. The bitterness of party strife led one faction to consider the other to be tyrannical, that is, seeking its own advantage at the expense of public welfare. Rienzo called the oligarchy of Rome *Tyrannicus* and the same epithet was applied in turn to his own dictatorship. Even in Tuscany, where the cities offered the longest resistance to the monarchical tendency, the identification of freedom and republicanism, autocracy and tyranny could not be maintained in the face of the great political changes going on by popular consent throughout central and northern Italy. Writers, whose general point of view was republican, were forced to admit that all *Signori* were not necessarily tyrants. Petrarch commended the government of both the Visconti and the Carraresi ; Matteo Villani, the historian of republican Florence, made an explicit distinction between *reali e naturali Signori* and tyrants.[1] It was inevitable that older concepts of tyranny should adjust themselves to the facts of signorial government and that lawyers and publicists should seek to deliver their cities from the evils of arbitrary power by working out new tests for despotic rule. As examples of the attempts of fourteenth-century thinkers to define the limits of signorial power, we shall consider the contributions of a lawyer and a

[1] Cf. Rienzo's recognition of Gonzaga of Mantua as a legitimate and constitutional ruler. In the Avogari lawsuit two witnesses stated that the Caminesi were *domini non naturales* or tyrants, because they had governed their subjects contrary to the law.

humanist politician, Bartolus of Sassoferato and Coluccio Salutati.

Bartolus was the first writer to state clearly the distinction between power unlawfully acquired and power unlawfully exercised. Though he repeats the Gregorian definition of the Tyrant as " he who does not rule the commonwealth according to law," he recognised that the acquisition of power raised quite a different question, as it related to the anticipation of misgovernment rather than to misgovernment itself. His consideration of the *tyrannus ex defectu tituli*, which on first reading seems of subsidiary importance to his distinction between the open, (*manifestus*), and the secret, (*tacitus et velatus*), tyrant, is, in fact, his main contribution to political theory. Its value lies in his examination of the defect in the *Signor's* title to rule, which he treats as arising out of a defective transfer of power ; a transfer that failed to be legally valid either through absence of the consent of the legal superior or through an imperfect declaration of the popular will. He gives four examples of defective transfers : (1) when a private person seizes and exercises power in a city which has not the right of appointing its governor ; (2) when a private person, through force, coerces a city, which has the right of appointment, into transferring jurisdiction to him; (3) when a governor or magistrate without legal authority prolongs his term of office beyond the period for which he was appointed ; (4) when a magistrate, under cover of one office, exercises supreme power over the city. The first two are examples of open and the second two of secret tyranny, but all four come under the general heading of *tyranni ex defectu tituli*. The first example shows the strength of the imperial tradition and reminds us that, *de iure*, almost all cities were legally subject to the Emperor and therefore were not fully competent to make a legal transfer of power, though they often enjoyed a limited right of appointing governors. The other three cases emphasise the necessity for the transfer of power to be a deliberate, voluntary act of the popular will, without any *vitium in consensu* due to violence or deceit. It follows that no one has, in himself, the right to govern ; his power must have its origin in an act of popular will in all parts complete and legally competent. The two essential factors in the transfer of power are the consent of the superior, freely given, and the consent of the majority of the citizens, freely acting. The tyrant *ex defectu tituli* is not, as earlier writers believed, he who overthrows a free constitution,[1] but he who seizes the government against the will of the governed. The people, subject to the consent of their legal superior, have the right and power to choose their own form of government.

Bartolus' treatment of the legally appointed ruler who governs unjustly, the *tyrannus exercitio*, is not so satisfactory. He enumerated ten signs of tyranny of this kind, taken from Plutarch ; of these the most important were the maintenance of factions in the city and the pauperisation and exploitation of the citizens. He added a corollary to the Trevisan judgment of 1314–15 by stating that contracts and other legal processes were invalid, if harmful to the citizens. He did not examine closely the question of tyrannicide and produced no definite juristic tests by which it could be decided at what moment the legitimate ruler becomes a tyrant, who shall judge him and what action may lawfully be taken against him. He was apparently content to lay the burden of deposing the *tyrannus exercitio* on his legal superior, though in practice neither papal nor imperial intervention was likely to occur. His concept of tyranny on this side shows that he was thinking more of the law than of the facts. His tractate would have been of small service to Milanese or Paduans

---

[1] E.g. Cornelius Nepos, *Miltiades*, c. 8, " omnes autem et dicuntur et habentur tyranni, qui perpetua potestate sunt in ea civitate quae perpetua libertate usa est."

who wished to depose one of the Visconti or Carraresi as *tyrannus exercitio*. In the same way he did not consider the case, which became fairly common later, in which a tyrant *ex defectu tituli* established a government, good in itself, which both subjects and superior might tacitly accept.[1] Though he wrote " hodie Italia est tota plena tyrannis," he seems to have regarded this as an abnormal phenomenon which could not persist. He looked forward to a time when all tyrannies would have passed away and did not take it upon himself to discuss the way in which they might be either regularised or abolished.

The Bartolian concept of tyranny was shaped more closely to the facts of Italian political conditions by Coluccio Salutati, a Florentine humanist and official, who wrote an epistolary tract entitled *De Tyranno* in the last decade of the fourteenth century.[2] The tract was addressed to his friend Master Antonio de Acquilo, student in arts at Padua, who had asked him a question much discussed by scholars, whether Dante was right to place Brutus and Cassius in the mouths of Satan. Though Coluccio's answer has considerable literary interest, both from its style and handling of classical material and as an interpretation of the last canto of the *Inferno*, its main value lies in its examination of the constitutional basis of organised society. In replying to Master Antonio, Colucci gave an answer to the general questions : when can we say that a government is a tyranny and in what circumstances is tyrannicide lawful ?

Coluccio repeated the Bartolian distinction between two kinds of tyranny, which he had probably discerned independently through study of the same sources. Like Bartolus, he refused to define tyranny as characteristic

---

[1] The Medici rule in Florence was a government of this kind.
[2] Coluccio was Florentine Secretary of State (*cancellarius*) from 1375 until his death in 1406. He was the first of the long line of humanist secretaries of the Florentine state.

of any one form of government, admitting that even a despotism was lawful, if the despot had a lawful title. He re-stated the theory of transfer of power and added to it the idea of tacit consent on the part either of the superior or of the people. A ruler who exercised untransferred authority over competent subjects was tyrant *ex defectu tituli*. Between competent, (i.e., sovereign), and incompetent subjects he recognised a new class of half-competent ; an act of transfer, made by them as completely as possible and not expressly revoked by their superior, was valid. Going further he admitted that the act of transfer need not be a formal public ceremony, but might consist in nothing more than the silent consent or acquiescence of the people.[1] The idea of tacit consent had not been expressed by Bartolus, though Marsilius of Padua had indicated it by the statement that a king could exercise lawful authority without being definitely elected by his subjects.[2] The notion that the Emperor by refraining from action might tacitly acknowledge the *Signor* and that the people might tacitly accept him by submitting to his rule, provided a justification for conditions as they actually existed and helped to show how many Italian *Signoria* developed out of irregular and informal organisations into sovereign states. Exercise of power, Coluccio maintained, carries with it its own legitimisation, since all government rests on consent. The full force of the idea of tacit consent can be seen when Coluccio's treatment of tyrannicide is examined. He admitted the right and even the duty of tyrannicide in the case of the tyrant *ex defectu*

---

[1] *De Tyranno*, II, § 8. " Forte tacitus ille consensus et obedientia, quoniam que per vim vel metum extorta sunt, resistentia quiescente, non sint irrita, sicut leges statuerunt, ipso iure, sequentique consensu tacito vel expresso purificentur et incipiant esse nec violenta nec meticulosa ; forte tacitus ille consensus, inquam, et obedientia tanti fuerit, quod, nisi prius superioris sententia contrarium declaretur, similitudinem iusti principis obtinebit."

[2] *Defensor Pacis*, 1, § 9.

tituli ; to kill him was no murder since he deserved to be treated as a murderer.[1]   But he definitely limited the right to slay the tyrant *exercitio* by refusing to the individual the right to condemn and punish his ruler.   The murder of Caesar by Brutus and Cassius was a criminal act, since no one may set his own judgment above the judgment of the community.   The tyrant *exercitio* can be condemned only by an orderly constitutional process ; his deposition and execution must be authorised by an act of popular sovereignty, expressing the will of the majority, and, if necessary, accompanied by the consent of the legal superior.[2] Even if Caesar had been a tyrant *exercitio*, his assassination could not be justified ; the crime was the more infamous as Caesar was no tyrant, but the lawful ruler of the Roman people, basing his authority on the will of his subjects.[3] Thus we find in the *De Tyranno* full recognition both of the medieval idea of popular sovereignty and of the modern idea of the legitimacy of any efficient *de facto* government. Coluccio saw the overpowering necessity of leadership so clearly that he was prepared to allow the *Signor* to justify himself by his works.   Though he retained his belief in the popular basis of power, examination of the facts and tendencies of contemporary politics led him to distrust its practical value.   " Nam et multorum regimen nihil est, nisi in unam sententiam conveniat multitudo : si quidem nisi percipiat unus et ceteri pareant, non unum erit, sed plura regimina . . . Natura quidem exigit ut, cum aliqui nati sint servire et aliqui principari, quoad

---

[1] *De Tyranno*, II, § 7.   Satis, ut arbitror, demonstratum est invadenti tyrannidem iure non a populi parte solum, sed a privato quolibet impune resisti posse, tale monstrum armis etiam cum cede et sanguine crudeliter opprimendo.

[2] *Ibid.*, II, § 24.   Non ponat igitur aliquis animam in manu sua, nec de voluntate sua faciat rationem et in dominum suum, licet etiam tyrannum se gerat, insurgat.   Autoritate superioris aut populi facienda sunt hec, non affectione propria presumenda.

[3] *Ibid.*, III, § 11.   Hic ne titulus Cesaris violentus atque tyrannicus, quem grata civitas tradidit ?

debite proportionis equalitas inter omnes observetur, ad meliorem perveniat principatus." [1] The opinion had often been expressed before ; [2] by its place in the context, Coluccio virtually admitted the necessity for a transfer of power from the people to the Signor.

Bartolus and Coluccio had developed a theory of tyranny in harmony with the facts of the fourteenth century. As we have seen, it had its origin in two fundamental ideas of the thirteenth century, the imperial idea and the idea of popular sovereignty, reconciled both in the doctrine that legitimate government must trace its origin to a transfer of power by the people, ratified by imperial consent, and in the person of the Signor, as representative of the power of the people and of the authority of the Emperor.[3] It can hardly come as a surprise that this theory was submerged in the maelstrom of war, policy, diplomacy, art and learning of fifteenth-century Italy. Political evolution could not halt at this stage of achievement. The withdrawal of the people from a share in the business of government, the atrophy of their political faculties and the emphasis on hereditary and territorial rights bestowed by legal superiors transformed the *Signoria*, based on popular consent, into a despotic principate or Tyranny. With the loss of the idea of popular sovereignty the juristic tests of the legitimacy of government ceased to have any meaning. It is true that Italian writers of the fifteenth century have much to say about tyranny and tyrannical government and that classical republicanism was discussed and even admired by humanists in many Italian cities. It is also true that in times of danger and

[1] *De Tyranno*, IV, §§ 15 and 16.
[2] By Aristotle, S. Thomas, Dante and Occam.
[3] The teaching of Bartolus and Coluccio about dominion under contract or transfer of power reappeared in the later sixteenth and in the seventeenth century. The apologists both of absolute monarchy and of Natural Right made it the keystone of their argument : the controversies between them turned on whether sovereignty lay with the prince or with the people when the transfer was complete.

panic the democratic tendency still expressed itself in assassination and revolution. These manifestations were only unsubstantial shadows of the lusty democracy of the earlier period. The life-giving idea of popular sovereignty had died of inanition ; there survived only the rhetoric of scholars, the doctrinaire artifices of ambitious politicians and the blind anger of frightened mobs. This degeneration of Italian republicanism can be illustrated either from the constitutional experiments or from the political writings of the last phase of Italian independence.

The constitutional changes in Florence after the expulsion of the Medici, (1494), showed how completely the idea of popular sovereignty had lost its force, even in the city that had the strongest tradition of republican government. Nothing illustrates more clearly the proposition that Italian constitutional development was an organic and not a revolutionary process than the gradual metamorphosis of the Florentine government. The Medici had not been destructive ; the old constitutional forms were maintained except for the substitution of a council of seventy, composed of supporters of the family, for the councils of the commune and of the *popolo*. Yet when Piero was driven out it immediately became plain that, deprived of the controlling influence of the Medici, the constitutional machine would not function. As the guilds and other party organisations had decayed, it was impossible to restore the earlier councils, and it was therefore necessary to draft a new constitution, (December 1494). The form of the new government and the speeches and sermons about it were highly significant. At first we seem to hear men speak again in the authentic voice of the fourteenth century and are almost constrained to believe, as the speakers did, that a great political renaissance had arrived. Savonarola preached : " The sole form of government suited to our needs is a civil and general government. Woe to thee, Florence, if thou

choosest a head to dominate and oppress all the rest. . . .
And let your first draft, or rather model and basis of government be conceived in such wise ; that no man may receive
any benefit save by the will of the whole people, who must
have the sole right of creating magistrates and enacting
laws." Luca Corsini, one of the most violent opponents
of the Medici, said in Council : " The Republic consists
of one body alone, and this body is the whole people,
which, unable itself to attend to every branch of administration, therefore appoints magistrates." When we examine
the constitution itself it is clear that the old phrases had
become the mere common form of political rhetoric. The
new government consisted of the old executive machinery
controlled by a *Consiglio Maggiore* in which sovereign powers
were vested. Persons eligible for membership were the
beneficiati or citizens over twenty-eight years of age who
had paid taxes and who had either held public office themselves or whose father, grandfather or great grandfather
had held that *beneficio*. As the size of the Council was not
to exceed 1,500 members, the *beneficiati* were divided into
three sections, each of which constituted the council for
a term of six months. Every three years sixty *non-beneficed*
citizens and young men of twenty-four were nominated
members of the Council, " in order to give encouragement
to the young and to incite them to virtue." The *beneficiati* were 3,200 in all ; as the total population of Florence
was then between 90,000 and 100,000, it is plain that
only a fraction of the inhabitants were enfranchised.
The drafters, while speaking the language of the past
were actually thinking of the strong oligarchy of Venice
and hoping to make their Council of *beneficiati* as efficient
as the Consiglio Maggiore of Venice. That they fully
realised the danger of democracy was shown by a law
passed six months later, (August 1495): " . . . It is
desired to maintain this government for ever, so that not
ourselves only, but also our children may enjoy this sacred

liberty, and that no one may dare to raise his head as a tyrant and subjugate free citizens ; it is also known that in no way can our liberty be so easily subverted and this new and good rule be overthrown as by means of the Parlamento. . . . The Magnificent Signory and Gonfalonier do hereby provide and ordain, that no parlamento be held in future—that henceforth the Signory shall swear never again to convoke one and that whoever may plot to do so shall be put to death and 3,000 florins be awarded to his denouncer." [1] The legislation was passed under the influence of Savonarola, who preached against the *Parlamento* in a way that recalls the speeches of Cromwell to his Parliaments. " I have taken thought of this Parlamento of thine and I hold it to be nought but a means of destruction, wherefore it were best to be rid of it. Come forward, my people ! Art thou not sole master now ? Yes ! See then that no *Parlamento* be called unless thou wouldst lose thy government. Know that the only purpose of the *Parlamento* is to snatch the sovereign power from the hands of the people. . . . And thou people, at the stroke of the bell calling thee to the *Parlamento*, rise and draw thy sword and ask—' What would'st thou ? Cannot the Council decide all things ? ' . . ." To the Florentine republicans democracy meant no more than a form of government that protected the community both from the tyranny of individuals and from popular anarchy. Their constitution was not an expression of the will of the people ; it was merely what Savonarola and his supporters believed to be the best government for the people.

The failure of the Florentine republican revival was regarded as the failure of democracy. Guicciardini, an observer who claimed to base his conclusions on " long experience and sound discretion," had nothing but contempt for it. " To speak of the people is to speak of madmen, for the people is a monster full of confusion and

[1] Cf. The closing of *Consiglio Maggiore* of Venice, 1297.

error and its vain beliefs are as far from truth as is Spain from India according to Ptolemy." Guicciardini was essentially a descriptive writer and we must turn to Machiavelli for a reasoned theory of the State. He also distrusted the people, though he found a subsidiary part for them in his ideal polity. In his historical writings even more than in *Il Principe*, he denied to democracy any creative force. Only the Prince or Legislator could give unity to society and bring the modern state into existence. His heroes—Theodoric, Castruccio Castracani and Cesare Borgia—were men who by native force surmounted all obstacles and established and organised the state. In the hands of the heroic leader the people were as white chalk in the hands of the draughtsman ; the function of subjects was merely to accept benefits bestowed on them and to guard them for their children. " The mass of men are better fitted to preserve a good government than to discover one for themselves."

PART II
THE STRUGGLE FOR SURVIVAL

CHAPTER VI

FEDERATION AND DEFENCE IN ITALY

INTRODUCTION: FEDERAL EXPERIMENTS IN ITALY.
ITALIAN MILITARY AND TERRITORIAL POLICY.

1. INTRODUCTION

THE key problem for the survival of the city state was its relation to its economic hinterland ; the larger and richer the city, the more important did this problem become. Even the small towns of the early Middle Ages could not subsist without a market for their goods and contributions of food stuffs and raw material from the countryside. As the population of the town increased, its area of rural influence was enlarged and its demand for country products became greater. Since the man-power of medieval armies came from the country, the military aspect of the problem presented equal difficulties. Urban communities soon lost military aptitudes and were unwilling to engage in war, even in their own defence, yet it became increasingly necessary to defend trade routes, defeat rival cities and resist the aggression of territorial rulers. In fact, though urban survival without rural co-operation was an impossibility, the whole trend of development was towards emphasising the exclusive individuality of the city and the difference between it and its hinterland. Cities attempted to solve the problem by forcing their peasant neighbours into a state of subjection. In Germany the *bann meilen recht* compelled peasants to supply to the cities necessities for industry, forbade the export of corn and raw material and created a monopoly relation between town and country. In Italy the cities conquered the *contado* and rigorously denied to its population, the *contadini*, any share in the privileges of citizenship. These efforts were not solutions of the problem ; they only served to accentuate hostility already existing and to increase the dangers of dislocation of trade and foreign invasion. The history of Venice shows how economic necessity and military dangers[1] forced a territorial policy on the ambitious city state and how not only country districts, but rival cities, were conquered and held subject. The alternatives seemed to be either absolute independence and oppression of others or subjection to a rival city or prince. Freeman [2] throws light on this dilemma by pointing out that an urban community can incorporate only within very narrow limits. " In such a commonwealth the city itself is everything. The representative system, by which all the inhabitants of a large country are enabled to have a share in the government, is not likely to occur to men's minds in such a state of things. Every citizen in a Democracy, every citizen of a ruling order in an Aristocracy, deems it his inalienable privilege to discharge his political functions in his own person. Consequently incorporation cannot be carried out over an extent of territory so large as to prevent the whole ruling body from habitually assembling in the city. . . . In short, among city commonwealths, where the Federal principle is not admitted,

---

[1] Fear of the aggression of Lombard tyrants, demand for food and raw material and the necessity of controlling the Alpine passes compelled Venice to adopt a policy of territorial conquest.

[2] *History of Federal Government in Greece and Italy.*

absolute political independence or absolute political subjection are the only alternatives."

Freeman has defined Federalism as "any union of component members, where the degree of union between the members surpasses that of mere alliance, however intimate, and where the degree of independence possessed by each member surpasses anything which can fairly come under the head of merely municipal freedom." This definition is essentially a historical definition and would not satisfy lawyers. Bryce, for example, defined the Federal State as that in which "the central government exercises direct power over the citizens of component communities." He denied the title of Federal State to any form of government known to exist before the constitution of the United States was established in 1788. For purposes of our inquiry the loose definition of Freeman is more satisfactory. He goes on to state two requisites necessary for a Federal Government in its perfect form. In the first place, each of the members of the Union must enjoy complete independence in those matters which concern each member only, as, for example, criminal jurisprudence or its political constitution. Secondly, all must be subject to a common power in matters which concern all members collectively, that is, in foreign policy, lines of communication, peace and war. The component members of a Federal Government are invested with every right of sovereignty on one class of subjects, but there is another class of subjects on which they are incapable of separate political action. "A Federal Union, in short, will form one State in relation to other powers, but many States as regards its internal administration."

We do not expect to find Federation as a common form of government in the later Middle Ages, because the prevalent constitutional tendency of the age was in the direction of unitary states, usually national monarchies. By the middle of the thirteenth century most of the monarchs of western Christendom were extending their jurisdiction, absorbing their smaller neighbours and establishing compact, centralised forms of organisation. The process showed that, normally, centripetal forces were stronger than centrifugal forces, or that the tendency which draws men or groups of men together in one organised community and keeps them there was stronger than the tendency which makes men or groups break away and disperse. In the national monarchy progress in the direction of a unitary state was maintained by setting various centripetal forces to work by means of common law, common law courts and common economic policy, and by reducing or regulating centrifugal forces through recognition of local variations and the exercise of physical force. England, for example, already was in possession of a representative parliament, law courts with law and procedure common to the whole realm and a uniform system of weights and measures ; her smaller neighbours, Ireland, Wales and Scotland, were being absorbed partly by conquest and partly by peaceful penetration.

In certain areas this general process was arrested or blocked by special circumstances which allowed centrifugal forces to remain too strong for the idea of a unitary state to develop. Such forces are usually most powerful in hilly or mountainous countries, where physical barriers prevent the free action of centripetal tendencies. The strength of local government forms evolved in Italy, the Alps and the Iberian peninsula during the early Middle Ages shows that geographical conditions played a large part in constitutional evolution. That geography, though important, was not a determining factor is proved by the ultimate appearance of a strong Spanish monarchy and by the number of highly developed political organisms, tenacious of independent life, which appeared in the level regions of the Netherlands and Lower Germany. The decisive influence was political. In Italy during the formative period, the weakness of and friction between the Papacy and the Empire checked the growth of central government. Within the Empire imperial preoccupations had caused a neglect of the organisation of centripetal forces. There was no national army, no national finance, no national justice and no national economic policy. Free play was given to the action of centrifugal forces, which found expression in the territorialism of the great feudatories, the colonisation of the eastern frontier and the Baltic coast, and the concentrated economic and political activities of the cities and the small communities of the Alps.

In spite of the strength of centrifugal tendencies in Italy and the Empire, the force of example and practical necessity were sufficiently potent to give rise to some movement towards unity in these countries. Such movements were almost bound by circumstances to assume a federal rather than a unitary form. The city state, as the history of Greece had already shown, adapted itself as naturally to federal organisation as it rebelled against amalgamation with its economic hinterland. Normally, hostility between urban and rural areas was too great to allow federations to assume any other form than leagues of cities. The cities recognised the economic and military dangers of isolation and hoped to find a remedy in alliances with units like themselves. Co-operation with country districts was usually either too difficult or too easy. If territorial rulers were strong, as in Germany, they sought to make cities their servants, rather than their allies ; if the rural population was weak and defenceless, as in Italy, the cities believed that only physical force was necessary to hold them in subjection. Only in Switzerland were town and country qualified to bargain on equal terms.

2. FEDERAL EXPERIMENTS IN ITALY

In Italy the principle of Federation was rejected after it had served the special purpose of organising resistance to the Hohenstaufen Emperors. The immediate cause of its adoption had been the attempt of Frederick Barbarossa to restore imperial authority in Lombardy. Like his contemporary, Henry II of England, Frederick was dominated by ideas of order, justice and legality ; he adopted theories of imperial power based on maxims of Roman Law, and applied them as the only remedy for the disorder caused by the vigorous expansion of the Lombard communes. He saw in Milan the centre of Lombard anarchy : in 1159 he besieged and captured it and forced the Milanese to recognise full imperial suzerainty and to guarantee the freedom of neighbouring cities. A general restoration of order had been attempted at the Diet of Roncaglia, (1158), at which Frederick, acting on the advice of Bolognese civilians, had resumed the *regalia* [1] and appointed imperial officers to govern the cities instead of the popularly elected Consuls. Frederick hoped by exercise of his legal rights to override the prescriptive autonomy of the cities. The effect of the new policy was to unite the communes against the Emperor. A series of leagues was formed, culminating in the Lombard League of 1167. Its chief members were Milan, Cremona, Brescia, Mantua, Ferrara, Venice, Verona, Vicenza, Padua and Treviso. Control was vested in Rectors, elected by the cities who belonged to the League, and all citizens were compelled to take oaths of obedience to these Rectors, to bind themselves to work for the common benefit, and to refrain from entering on peace or war without the League's consent. Through the efforts of the League, Milan was rebuilt, Alessandria was founded and the imperial army was defeated at Legnano, (1176). Frederick was forced to withdraw the decrees of Roncaglia, (1177), and, by signing the Treaty of Constance, (1183), to recognise the rights of the communes to elect their own magistrates, [2]

[1] i.e., profits of justice, appointment of officials, mints, tolls, etc.
[2] The Emperor retained the power of investing the consuls with their official dignity and of exercising appellate jurisdiction.

to erect fortifications and to retain their ancient tolls and customs. After the Treaty of Constance the Lombard League fell to pieces and the old conditions of rivalry and war between the communes reappeared.

The movement for the emancipation of central Italy was almost half a century later than that of Lombardy. The Florentine revolt of 1119 had been premature and it was not until the death of Henry VI, (1197), that imperial vicars ceased to exercise authority in Tuscany and Umbria. The Emperor's heir was a child, (afterwards Frederick II), and it soon became clear that the imperial system in Central Italy could no longer be held together. Under the direction of Florence, a League of Tuscan cities was formed against the Empire. The main terms of the alliance were confederation for common defence against all opponents of the League and a pledge that no peace or truce should be made with any Emperor, King, Prince, Duke or Marquis without the consent of the Rectors of the League. It was not organised to meet any special danger, but simply to take advantage of the death of Henry VI to secure for the cities the complete possession of their respective territories. Innocent III became an avowed champion of the League, even consenting that communes over which he claimed jurisdiction should become members. Resistance to it was purely local and within a decade the last vestige of imperial authority had disappeared in Tuscany.

The Emperors were never able to re-establish the system of government which had been overthrown by the Lombard and Tuscan Leagues. Frederick II made a bold attempt to govern Italy on a federal basis, dividing the whole of northern and central Italy into five or six vicariates under an imperial legate. The cities were then so exhausted by faction fighting and civil war that they made little resistance and, if it had not been for the determined hostility of the Papacy, Frederick might have succeeded in establishing a monarchical despotism in Italy. When

Frederick died in 1250 his descendants were destroyed by the Guelf or Papalist party and all hope of an Italian federation perished in the embittered rivalries of the later Guelf and Ghibelline wars. After the fall of the Hohenstaufen serious danger from foreign invaders came to an end and the most urgent motive for federation as a means of defence disappeared. Commercial and territorial competition between one city and another destroyed the basis of confidence and good-will necessary for permanent union. The renewal of foreign dangers at the end of the fifteenth century came too late : by that time local variations and jealousies had become so stereotyped that the cities and principalities of Italy found submission to a foreign enemy easier than confederation with each other.

An isolated project of Italian federation was proposed by Rienzo in 1347. His foreign policy was dominated by the idea of a grand Italian Federation, by means of which good government should be established and peace maintained throughout the peninsula. With this end in view, he wrote letters and sent embassies to all the chief cities and tyrants of Italy. He proposed that each Italian city and principality should preserve its own laws, administration and independence, though all should be united together in a federal bond. Rome was to be the headquarters of the League ; in Rome would meet an assembly in which all cities of importance were represented. The functions of this assembly would be to arbitrate in quarrels between members of the Federation, to enquire into questions of public order and to represent Italy in negotiations with foreign powers. Later, he thought the election of Emperors would be a suitable function for this assembly. As a supplement to it, there was to be a supreme Judicial Tribunal, composed of the ablest jurisconsults in Italy, to which appeal could be made about difficult legal questions. He proposed, in short, to establish a sort of League of Nations for Italy, which would put an end to war in the peninsula and organise national order and defence. In order to carry out his design, Rienzo entered into negotiations with the chief cities and principalities of Italy. Envoys were sent to him by all the Tuscan cities, by Venice and by the tyrants of North Italy. A measure of support was then ensured and it is possible that the design might have been put to the proof if Rienzo had succeeded in maintaining his prestige and power. His actions showed him to be deficient in judgment, knowledge of politics and diplomatic skill. He failed to realise the necessity of placating the Roman nobles and maintaining friendly relations with the Papacy. His morale was destroyed by the vertigo of success, and he seems to have suffered from a form of megalomania. The extent of his designs and the essential weakness of his character were revealed by the elaborate ceremony with which he was made knight, (August 1, 1347). He took the bath of knighthood in the font of S. John's Lateran, where the Emperor Constantine was said to have been baptised. Afterwards he appeared before a vast crowd of Romans and, in a proclamation made by his notary, assumed the titles—" Liberator of Rome : Defender of the Rights of Italy : August Tribune : Protector of the Human Race." It was announced at the same ceremony that in the opinion of the most eminent jurisconsults, all rights of possession, jurisdiction and sovereignty once enjoyed by Rome still belonged to her. In virtue of these rights and of the absolute power freely committed to him by the Romans, Rienzo declared that the right of electing the Emperor belonged to Rome and Italy. " Rome is the capital of the whole world and the sanctuary of the Christian faith ; all cities and peoples of Italy are and shall be free ; we grant to all the inhabitants of holy Italy the rights and privileges attached to the title of Roman citizens." When the proclamation was read Rienzo stretched out his sword in three directions saying " This is mine, this is mine, this is mine."

The proclamation shows that Rienzo's design was nothing less than the restoration, under his own dictatorship, of the Roman Empire. The federal project was dropped in favour of the incorporation of all the people of Italy as citizens of Rome. There can hardly be any doubt that he hoped to make himself Emperor. His political schemes became a mere humanist extravaganza and his followers deserted him in consternation ; the Italian cities and the Papacy withdrew their support ; he was excommunicated and, two days later, was expelled from Rome by the troops of the nobles, (December 14, 1347). His federal project was soon forgotten and was without influence on the policy of Italian states.

3. ITALIAN MILITARY AND TERRITORIAL POLICY

The fall of the Hohenstaufen and the renunciation of Italian ambitions by Rudolf of Habsburg brought to an end the danger of Teutonic domination, against which Italy had been struggling intermittently since the collapse of the Roman Empire. Peace did not follow the end of the German peril. The cities which had fought for the Guelf or Ghibelline cause used the old names to cover new ambitions and turned their energies to enlarging their frontiers at the expense of their neighbours. Two centuries of internecine war followed ; the motive forces were the land hunger of Verona, Milan, Naples and the Papacy and the commercial greed of Venice, Florence, Pisa and Genoa. New conditions of warfare developed to correspond to new motives for war and to changes in the social condition of the combatants. In the twelfth and thirteenth centuries the communes fought their own battles. The *Grandi* formed the cavalry arm ; the *Popolo* composed the infantry ; cavalry and infantry went into battle together, bringing with them the *caroccio* or chariot bearing the banners of the commune. The infantry or civic militia had a certain measure of military training and were sufficiently well-disciplined to execute manœuvres in the field and to co-operate with the cavalry. It was by use of forces of this kind that the cities won their independence.

At the end of the thirteenth century a variety of circumstances combined to bring about the decline of urban militarism and the rise of mercenary armies. As commerce and industry developed, the civic militia decayed ; citizens were too much preoccupied with money-making to spend their time in military training. The *Grandi* diminished in number and the communes were less and less willing to use them as cavalry. Urban governments preferred to hire mercenaries rather than to give dangerous opportunities to the *Grandi* or to harass the bourgeoisie by conscription. The long wars of the Guelfs and Ghibellines had provided the material out of which mercenary armies could be formed. Political exiles, ruined by forfeitures, German soldiers, who came to Italy in the train of an imperial candidate, other foreign adventurers from France and Spain could fairly easily be enlisted under the banner of any military commander with a reputation for generosity and good luck. These *condottieri* armies give to Italian history of the later Middle Ages a confused impression of incessant movement and disorder. The opportunism of their leaders, the random way in which they seem to be employed, their marches, raids and countermarches combine to form a sort of moving picture of an indefinite number of powerful generals, whose armies brought anarchy and disaster to every city and principality which employed them. In reality great *condottieri* leaders were few and it is fairly easy to indicate the range of their activities.[1]

[1] *Vide* Sir Charles Oman : *The Art of War.* (New edition, Vol. II, Book XII.). The history of the great *condottieri* falls into three phases :

1. The first Italian *condottieri* period, *c.* 1338–*c.* 1360. These armies operated mainly in Tuscany and the Papal States.

2. The transalpine mercenary period, 1360–*c.* 1389. Disbanded

The great Italian *condottieri* period (*c.* 1378–*c.* 1494) might be said to begin with the outbreak of the great Schism. When the Italian Pope Urban VI found himself opposed by the Antipope Clement VII and the French cardinals, he took into his pay Alberigo of Barbiano, a count of the Romagna and founder of the *condottieri* army known as the Company of S. George. Clement VII was supported by a similar force of Bretons, commanded by his nephew, Count Montjoie. Thus even in military affairs, the Schism took on a national character. When, in 1379, the Company of S. George defeated the Bretons within sight of Rome Urban presented them with a banner bearing the inscription *Italy delivered from the barbarians*. Before the end of the century native *condottieri* had completely superseded the foreign companies from over the Alps. The chief factor in the new development was the Company of S. George. " For thirty years," Sir Charles Oman writes, " Alberigo took his band round Italy, serving sometimes Naples and sometimes Milan with great success. . . ." His army became the great military school of Italy. Italian governments recognised that the Italian soldier was the equal of the foreigner and Italian *condottieri* armies were recruited freely from all classes of society. In the Company of S. George the great military leaders of the fifteenth century were trained ; of these the greatest were Braccio di Montone and Attendola Sforza. Their fortunes illustrate in different ways the new capacities and potentialities of the *Condottieri* movement. During the first two phases the *condottieri* were nomadic ; in time of war they lived on the march or in quarters provided by the government that employed them ; in time of peace they subsisted by brigandage.

soldiers from the French wars served in Lombardy and central Italy They were not numerous enough for conquest ; their leaders, though greedy, were not ambitious ; their chief importance was the stimulus they gave to the *condottieri* habit.

3. The second Italian *condottieri* period, *c.* 1378–1494.

Their captains were content with the rewards of plunder and were not politically ambitious. Men like Monreale or Hawkwood would rather pillage cities than rule them. Changed conditions in Italy changed the attitude of *condottieri* commanders. As princes and cities consolidated their authority, it became increasingly difficult to maintain armies by brigandage. Almost every village was equipped for defence and fortresses were built at all important strategic points. There were four hundred fortified places in the state of Florence alone. The wealth of Italian governments made the work of fortification fairly simple and, owing to the slow development of artillery warfare, the art of defence tended to checkmate the science of attack. As a result, the problems confronting a leader of *condottieri* altered in character. He could no longer expect to pay his troops by pillage and was forced to seek some other means of maintaining them when not in employment. The Venetians for a time engaged a standing army of mercenaries, but this practice was not general. The *condottieri* leaders adopted the solution of capturing for themselves a city or group of cities which would serve as permanent military bases. Thus Braccio conquered and held Perugia between 1416 and 1424; about the same time Attendola Sforza held many strong places in the kingdom of Naples and in the Papal States; his son, Francesco Sforza, became first Marquis of Ancona and then Duke of Milan. Other leaders like Colleone, Carmagnola, and Gattamelata amassed immense fortunes by securing continuous employment in the service of wealthy cities like Venice or Milan. Under the direction of men of great ambition and powers of organisation the professional soldier ceased to be an undisciplined brigand and in the fifteenth century professional armies became a regular and ordered part of Italian social structure.

The military value of *condottieri* armies has been the cause of some controversy. Humanist historians at the beginning of the sixteenth century agreed in denouncing the ineffectiveness and cowardice of *condottieri* troops and their opinion has been accepted with very little hesitation by many modern writers.   To understand the reason why Italian armies were unable to resist transalpine troops during the second period of invasion a brief examination of the subject on the technical side is necessary.   It should be remembered that until the end of the fifteenth century the reputation of Italian generals stood high and Italy was regarded as a training place in the art of war.   It is not enough to accept the statements of writers like Machiavelli, who explained the military weakness of Italy by decrying the idea of a professional army and abusing *condottieri* officers as cowardly and treacherous.

Owing to special circumstances, Italian commanders were not aware of the importance of military changes north of the Alps.   In the fourteenth century English archers and Swiss pikemen demonstrated the superiority of well-armed and disciplined infantry over cavalry.   The battles of Morgarten and Creçy were the beginning of a general change from shock tactics, combined with close cavalry fighting, to missile tactics, combined with close infantry fighting.   In the century after Creçy the armies of northern Europe began to be reconstituted to satisfy changed conditions and feudal cavalry became less and less important. In Italy the older method of warfare was retained.   After the decline of the communal militia in the second half of the thirteenth century, infantry was not much used in Italian warfare, though the companies of foreign adventurers, who came to the peninsula after the treaty of Bretigny, re-introduced the sytem.   Sir John Hawkwood was a master of the new tactics and proved in a series of engagements the value of dismounted men-at-arms and archers.   But English infantry were too few and French infantry too sceptical of the value of the new method to bring about a change.   Italian infantry were, for the most part, cross-bowmen ; against their slow and ineffective bolts the heavy armour of the cavalry man was an adequate protection. In France and Switzerland cavalry had been routed by the long bow and the pike, but there was no corresponding development of infantry equipment in Italy. Moreover, infantry troops, to be efficient, must be highly trained. Italian civic militias had no such training partly because tyrants and oligarchs were afraid of the democratic tendency of a permanent military force. The citizens themselves were unwilling to submit to training and the *contadini* were not loyal enough to be trusted. The fluctuating size of armies gave *condottieri* generals little time for the effective training of infantry ; the great Italian commanders were all, without exception, cavalry men.[1] It is, therefore, not surprising that, in the third period of *condottieri* history, there was a general reversion to cavalry fighting.

Cavalry fighting was not really suited to Italian geography and it imposed serious limitations on the scope of military operations. Much of the country was either marshy or mountainous land in which cavalry battles could not be fought. The plain country of Lombardy and southern Venetia was cut up by irrigation channels which mounted troops were bound to avoid. Military operations could not be carried on in the winter months and in the spring and summer they were limited to roads and open country. The result was that manœuvres, marches and counter-marches became of overwhelming importance. All the skill and energy of a *condottieri* general was concentrated on the task of " getting the enemy into such a position that he could not attack with advantage.

---

[1] One reason for the persistence in the use of cavalry has been clearly and, perhaps, over-emphatically stated by Machiavelli. Cavalry troops were more spectacular and could be displayed before employers to better advantage. " A moderate following of horsemen was thought to confer distinction and could be more easily maintained." (*Il Principe.*)

The weaker side manœuvred with the object of placing itself behind obstacles. . . . The stronger side . . . endeavoured to outflank and dislodge the enemy by circular movements of great length. . . . Then the weaker side had to get away in haste and seek for another "*blocking*" position, from which it would, in due time, be evicted once more. A whole campaign might be a bloodless series of manœuvres for position, with no definite result " (Sir Charles Oman : *Art of War*). These manœuvres, rendered necessary by the nature of the country and the composition of armies,[1] were frequently misunderstood by non-combatants. Fabian tactics are seldom popular and often arouse suspicions of timidity and treachery. Hence the bitter criticism of as acute a civilian observer as Machiavelli : " The *condottieri* spared no endeavour to relieve themselves and their men of fatigue and danger, not slaying one another in battle, but making prisoners, who were afterwards released without ransom." A German historian, Doctor Willibald Block, has recently, (1913), undertaken an investigation of the general charge of avoiding fatigue and danger which has been brought against *condottieri* troops since the time of Machiavelli. He has shown that older methods of computing losses in the field were unsatisfactory, as they were based on misunderstandings about the size and composition of *condottieri* armies. He refuses to accept Machiavelli's denunciations of *condottieri* armies and explains their military failures by reference to other causes. He concludes : " At the end of the fifteenth century we have a complete revolution in military science. . . . As the main line of defence, infantry took the

[1] Another cause of long-drawn-out warfare was the failure to recognize the value of artillery. The traditions of military science had become stereotyped ; fortification was the art of defence, blockade and the cavalry charge the art of attack. Machiavelli himself did not perceive the value of artillery, but limited the use of cannon to giving a loud salvo as a signal that the battle had begun.

place of mounted men of arms and the close tactical formation of infantry replaced the open field order of the knights. Partly through the ferocity of the Swiss, partly through the light defensive armour of this new infantry and partly through the better fire arms which were coming more and more into use, casualties in the field were considerably increased. As a result of these changes the Italians, at a disadvantage against other nations, in spite of the personal bravery of their knights and mercenaries, collapsed and were conquered. . . ." Machiavelli's explanation of Italian military disasters is, in fact, much too facile. Like most civilian critics of military operations, he is inclined to blame the morale of the troops for reverses which were due primarily to more technical causes. Italian armies were not unmilitary, but old-fashioned. Their commanders had failed to realise the new importance of infantry, mainly because the political and territorial organisation of Italy made the training of an effective infantry force almost an impossibility. They believed that by getting rid of the feudal organisation and discipline of cavalry troops they had brought their armies to the highest state of efficiency. They did not realise that, in warfare, it was not feudalism, but cavalry that had been discredited.

The ultimate consequence of the back-water tactics and strategy of *condottieri* generals was the collapse of Italian resistance to foreign invaders and the conquest of the peninsula by transalpine armies. As Machiavelli puts it, " Charles of France was suffered to conquer Italy with chalk." The armies that began to cross the Alps in 1494 were professional armies, like the *condottieri* themselves, but they were the armies of kings, recruited throughout a countryside, not the property of their captains. By them the tactics of the pike and musket were developed as the logical consequence of the lesson of the pike and the long bow. Italy, in spite of incessant fighting, had failed to learn the lesson and the collapse of Italian armies in the field was inevitable. This failure was in turn due to the general policy of Italian governments, which, by oppressing conquered areas and releasing citizens from military service, made the recruiting and training of an effective infantry force impossible.

Italian cities governed subject towns and provinces with varying degrees of severity, but in no case did the sovereign city confer on its dependents a share in her own supreme controlling power. Venice granted greater freedom to her subjects than any other city, yet her dominion was feared more than that of any other state in Italy. Though local customs and local institutions were left unchanged, the loss of political liberty remained a root of bitterness, which even a full share in the economic prosperity of the Republic could not destroy. The Florentines treated conquered areas with greater distrust and severity. As Villari says, " The spectacle of a Pisan or a Pistoian in the Councils of the Florentine republic would have been as extraordinary as nowadays that of a citizen of Paris or Berlin seated on the benches of the Italian parliament." The treatment meted to Pisa after her annexation in 1406 illustrates the extremes to which Italian methods of coercive expansion could be carried.[1] The Florentines were determined to render impossible any revival of the agriculture and commerce on which the prosperity of the city had been based. Agriculture in the Arno delta had been developed by means of an elaborate system of drainage and irrigation. The canals and dikes were now allowed to fall into ruin ; as a result stagnant water rendered tillage impossible and bred fevers noxious to the inhabitants. Pisan commerce and industry were destroyed by direct prohibition. It was decreed that no citizens of Pisa should engage either in the manufacture

[1] *Vide* J. S. C. Bridge : *A History of France from the Death of Louis XI.* (Vol. II, pp. 145-7).

of silk and wool or in any wholesale trade. The same spirit of coercion prevailed in political policy ; the Florentines knew nothing of Burke's " commercial servitude and civil liberty." The Pisans were excluded from all public office, over-loaded with taxes and exposed to private extortion of every kind. It is not surprising that the arrival of Charles VIII in 1494 was a signal for revolt. The streets rang with shouts of " France and Liberty " ; Florentine soldiers and officials were hunted from the city. A colonial policy of this kind made impossible any system of defence based on recruiting of troops in subject provinces or cities.

Guicciardini observed that it was an axiom of politics that a republic " grants no share of its grandeur to any but the citizens of its chief city, while oppressing all the others. . . ." For this reason the city state in Italy never became an organic unity ; the canker which destroyed it was its refusal to admit conquered subjects to citizenship. In attempting to build up a theory of the state and to determine the means by which social unity might be achieved, Machiavelli fastened on the territorial policy of republics as the radical cause of their weakness. " Republics," he wrote in the second book of the *Discorsi*, ' have three modes of aggrandising their states : first, by confederation among themselves on the Etruscan or Swiss plan : [1] secondly, by placing the conquered on the same footing with themselves . . . which was the plan pursued by the Romans ; thirdly, by creating subjects and not associates, as did the Spartans and the Athenians. The third method is of all the worst, since to undertake to hold and govern cities by violence, especially those which have been used to freedom, is a difficult and wearisome

---

[1] Machiavelli rejected the federal method because he believed it was unsuited to a policy of conquest. He failed to see that the admission of rural cantons to the confederation as members equal to the cities was the great achievement of the Swiss.

matter. . . . Aggrandisement by the subjection and oppression of subjects is a system that proved injurious even to armed republics like Sparta and Athens, and will always be ruinous to unarmed republics like ours. The truest and best method then is that pursued by the Romans of creating, not subjects, but comrades. . . ."

CHAPTER VII

FEDERATION AND DEFENCE IN GERMANY

IMPERIAL POLICY. LEAGUES IN SOUTHERN AND WESTERN GERMANY. THE HANSEATIC LEAGUE.

1. IMPERIAL POLICY

CONDITIONS in Italy were abnormal. The absence of foreign intervention for a long period and the great wealth of many of the cities postponed the necessity for union and hid the fact that small independent political units live dangerously. North of the Alps, where cities were neither rich enough nor secure enough to stand alone, a series of federal experiments was undertaken. The chief obstacle was the existence of unitary states, the national monarchies or principalities where a centralised government was already organised on a territorial basis. If the federated cities were to maintain themselves it was necessary that they should be in possession of an adequate military force, economic freedom and control over their hinterlands. Swiss cities alone were able to fulfil all three conditions and they alone were victorious in the struggle for survival. German cities allowed all their attention to be absorbed by the task of protecting commerce ; they failed to produce a permanent solution of the problem of survival because they failed in territorial policy. The failure was due partly to pressure from without and partly to indifference. The movement for emancipation had never been as vigorous in Germany as in Italy, chiefly because it had not been directed against foreigners. As a result the cities were out-witted and out-manœuvred by Emperors and princes imbued with the Teutonic concept of territorial rather than urban units of government. The issue was decided against the cities in the thirteenth century, though the consequences were not clear for more than two hundred years later.

Imperial authority had dual foundations. Its sanction and permanence were based upon the medieval belief in the necessity of a universal sovereign who should bring order and harmony to the whole Christian Commonwealth. But the universal sovereign was also king of Germany; his strength ultimately depended upon his control over the resources of his kingdom. By the middle of the tenth century Germany had become a feudal monarchy. The king was titular lord of the soil; he could exact from his vassals money and military service, allocate vacant fiefs and wage war at his pleasure. These rights were feudal rights, created by a whole series of private bargains, assigning functions and status to particular persons and guaranteeing to them legal security. The monarch was limited in the exercise of his rights by the reciprocal duties he owed to his vassals and by the practical difficulty of enforcing them against powerful feudatories. Thus from the first the autocratic authority of the Emperor was checked and thwarted by his status as feudal King.

Bryce [1] has pointed out that the Emperors were forced to struggle unsuccessfully against the three principles of nationality, aristocracy and popular government. Their struggles against nationality ended in the emancipation of France, Poland, Hungary, Denmark, Burgundy and Italy. Aristocracy in the form of feudalism, destroyed their effective strength in Germany during and after the Great Interregnum, (1250–73). In Italy and in the Alps the free cantons successfully defended the right of popular

[1] *The Holy Roman Empire*, pp. 433–4.

government against the Emperors. It is with the imperial struggle against popular government that we are concerned and here it is impossible to discover a consistent policy. The same monarch who tried to crush the communes of Lombardy and Tuscany favoured the rise of free towns in Germany and, intermittently, protected the liberties of the Alpine cantons. The difference in policy was determined by circumstances. The struggle in Italy was due to the investiture contest and the absence of a strong territorial nobility. North of the Alps the Emperors showed no hostility towards free self-government until the triumph of the feudal aristocracy in the thirteenth century forced them to adopt territorialism as the basis of their authority.

From the tenth to the beginning of the thirteenth century the growth of German cities was encouraged by the Emperors, sometimes by grants of market rights and charters and sometimes by foundation. The Hartz towns owed their rise to the Saxon Emperors and Lübeck was protected and developed by Barbarossa and Frederick II. In southern and western Germany numerous towns grew up under the protection of Salian and Hohenstaufen Emperors. Frederick I attached them to the crown by grants of municipal institutions, independent jurisdiction and privileges of exemption. Suabia alone contained forty free towns which later became *Reichstädte* or imperial cities. Through this policy a third estate of free cities arose in Germany, which, if other conditions had been favourable, might have saved the monarchy.

A change in imperial policy was begun by Frederick II. By the thirteenth century the long wars in Italy and Germany had increased the power of all feudatories, both secular and ecclesiastical, and the Emperor was compelled to admit quasi-autonomy within their territories. To conciliate the bishops he tried, (1220), to restore their authority over the cities in their dioceses, pledging himself to refuse citizenship in imperial cities to subjects who had left the service of an ecclesiastical prince, to prohibit the erection of castles or cities on church land without the consent of the lord of the land and to grant no new tolls or mints within the territory or jurisdiction of any prince without his consent. Further edicts issued by Frederick II show that he was prepared to promise his help to the princes to check the expansion of the cities. The special grievances of the territorial nobility were commercial and industrial monopolies, extension of civic jurisdiction and absorption of immigrants. In 1231 Frederick issued an edict in favour of the princes which was almost a Charter of Liberties for the aristocracy of Germany. No new castles or cities were to be erected to the prejudice of local landholders ; no new markets were to interfere with the profits of older markets. Lands and fiefs of princes, nobles, officials and churches, which had been acquired by cities, were ordered to be restored. The jurisdiction of the cities was limited and they were commanded to expel *Phalburgii* [1] and to refuse citizenship to serfs and criminals seeking refuge behind their walls. These and other clauses diminished the rights of the crown, increased the power of territorial lords and blocked the expansion of the cities. A further decree, issued in the same year, interfered in the internal government of cities. All civic officials who held office without the consent of their bishop were deposed ; all guilds or corporations were dissolved ; all privileges and charters granted in the past to the disadvantage of the princes or of the Empire were revoked and declared invalid.

Neither the princes nor the Emperor were strong enough to enforce these decrees. Enough was done to arrest the territorial expansion of the cities, but it was some time before the full effect of the policy was understood.

---

[1] Phalburgii or pfalburgii were persons or corporations dwelling outside cities, but enjoying political rights within them.

In spite of all prohibitions, the cities continued to admit serfs to citizenship and to bestow burgher rights on persons dwelling in the country. Following the medieval axiom, " no law without exception," the Emperors themselves were not consistent in their policy of abandoning the cities to the princes. Even Frederick II exempted favoured places from his general edicts : in 1236 he granted to the citizens and *Phalburgii* of Strassburg the right to refuse services and taxes to all feudatories and in 1245, in spite of the obstinate resistance of the bishop, he gave Regensburg the right to elect its own municipal officers. After the Interregnum Rudolf of Habsburg allied himself with the merchant aristocracy against the princes, raised many of them to knightly rank and used them as his ministers. His immediate successors—Adolf, Albert and Henry VII —showed less favour to the cities, but when war broke out between Frederick of Habsburg and Lewis of Bavaria, (1314), the latter won the support of the Suabian Patriciate by large concessions to Jews and merchants.[1] Lewis was the last Emperor to make a serious effort to use the cities in the work of maintaining order and furthering imperial policy. The Luxemburg and later Habsburg Emperors were too much absorbed in purely territorial aggrandisement to carry on his work. It is significant that the only clause relating to the towns in the Golden Bull was a reiteration of Frederick II's restriction of *Phalburgii*. In the last quarter of the fourteenth century a series of conflicts broke out between the cities of Upper Germany and their territorial lords. Though the princes were victorious in the field, the cities retained control of their internal affairs. The triumph of territorialism was postponed until the Reformation. The economic and political

---

[1] Numerous letters are extant which were sent by Lewis to the towns explaining his policy and asking for their support. He also encouraged the towns to co-operate with other estates to enforce *Landfrieden*.

development of the cities continued, but they withdrew more and more from national life and showed themselves indifferent to all public issues in which they had not a direct interest. Maximilian. summed up their general attitude in a sentence : " If a merchant loses a sack of pepper, he wants me to call the whole Empire to arms, but when there is business on hand, which concerns all Germany, the principalities and the Church, then no one can win the support of the cities."

2. LEAGUES IN SOUTHERN AND WESTERN GERMANY

As we have already seen, commerce was of predominant importance for German cities, nearly all of which lay on trade routes and were distributing centres for local manufacturers, raw material and foreign imports. Protection of commerce by land and water became the governing factor in the foreign policy of almost every city. Grand commerce was always precarious, as it ultimately depended on the favours and privileges granted by foreign rulers. German commerce was tied at both ends. Its oriental wares were imported from Italy and distributed to the kingdoms of the north and west and the bulk of its raw material came from the plains of Russia and Poland. Friendly relations with all these powers were necessary to the prosperity of German cities. A war with Venice threw the whole trade of upper Germany into confusion ; a war with the Scandinavian powers blocked the entrance to the Baltic and threatened the safety of German merchantmen ; a war with Poland interrupted communications with the markets of the Russian plain. Like the Venetians in Constantinople German merchants were always seeking for the position of the " most favoured nation " in the countries on which they relied for their exports and imports. Within the frontiers of Germany lines of communication were so long that the pack-trains and barges of merchants were in constant danger of attack by robbers or marauding armies. Even if a first-class war between the Emperor and the princes was not in progress, private war between neighbours was almost incessant. The growing power of the princes was steadily reducing the knights or lesser land-holders to a condition of poverty which virtually compelled them to supplement the revenue of their small estates by plunder. As there was no effective system of police and no public law for the whole social order, the knights, either spasmodically or as a regular profession, enriched themselves at the expense of merchant caravans. In the north piracy was rife along the whole coast line of the North Sea and the Baltic. Pirate gangs were recruited in Scandinavia, Frisia, Flanders and Lower Germany; their leaders were usually knights who found a freebooter's life at sea more profitable than brigandage on land. The petty nobility of Frisia and north-east Germany often invested all their fortunes in fitting out pirate ships in the hope of making a quick profit at the expense of the cities. The robber knights of the south and the pirate chiefs of the north carried on the Viking tradition of plunder and adventure in a degraded form, never aiming at conquest or commerce, but giving all their energy to spoils and destruction.

In such circumstances it was fairly clear that treaties, financial privileges and defence of lines of communication were essential to the prosperity of German commerce. The cities soon realised they were too weak to make individual bargains and too poor to police the highways of commerce. As there was no territorial power in Germany strong enough to protect their interests, they began to co-operate with each other in order to make treaties, secure privileges, black-list defaulters and share the expense of protecting trade routes. These Leagues were a direct consequence of the failure of the central government to secure public order; they began to develop during the last years of the reign of Frederick II. Unlike the Lombard League or the Confederation of Swiss Cantons, they had no immediate political purpose, but arose out of the struggle for economic survival. If the Post-Interregnum Emperors had been able to restore order and to protect German commerce at home and abroad, the German Leagues of cities would probably have had no more than episodic interest.

The earliest of these were the Rhine Leagues of the thirteenth century.[1] In 1247, under the leadership of Mainz about sixty cities of Upper Germany entered into a protective alliance. In 1254 Mainz, Cologne, Worms, Speyer, Strassburg and Bâle renewed their former confederation and drew up a formal statement of conditions of membership. No military undertakings were to be entered upon without the consent of the League and then only for a necessary defensive purpose ; no member of the League might furnish arms or give credit of loans to any common enemy ; all members were to keep themselves prepared for war. The cities between the Moselle and Bâle bound themselves to provide a hundred ships of war manned by archers and the cities below the Moselle five times as many.[2] Each member sent to sessions of the League four official representatives, who had full authority to act for their cities in all common business. In 1256 it was decided that diets or sessions should be held four times a year and that a judicial tribunal should be established to arbitrate in disputes between members. The League did good work during the Interregnum by protecting commerce in the Rhineland but, though it included almost a hundred cities and was supported by the Rhenish episcopate and many local landlords, it failed to maintain itself for long. It revived again for a

[1] Lübeck and Hamburg formed an alliance to protect their citizens from robbery in 1241 ; out of it the Hanseatic League developed. *Vide* § 3.

[2] All ferries except those near cities of the League were to be destroyed, in order that enemies of the League might be deprived of means of crossing the Rhine.

time in the fourteenth century, but never acquired any permanent political or economic importance.

In southern Germany the need for protection was equally great and from the beginning of the fourteenth century leagues were organised to maintain peace and public order. At first these Leagues were organisations to enforce *Landfrieden* or general agreements of all classes to keep the peace and punish evil-doers throughout the country. In 1331, for example, a *Landfriede* pact was signed at Ulm by all the chief cities and princes of Bavaria and Suabia. As discord between the cities and the princes increased, the two parties drew away from each other and began to form separate confederations. In 1349 Ulm and Augsburg organised a league of twenty-five imperial cities to defend their liberties.[1] After the publication of the Golden Bull, (1356), which blocked expansion by prohibiting the exercise of jurisdiction over *Phalburger* or non-resident citizens, the separatist tendency grew stronger. Charles IV was, on the whole, unfriendly to the cities, but he had sufficient influence to prevent open war. When he was succeeded by the incompetent Wenceslas, (1376), both cities and princes arranged their forces and prepared for a decisive encounter.

The Suabian League was founded in 1376. Acting on the initiative of Ulm, fourteen imperial cities in Suabia concluded an alliance to keep the peace and maintain their independence against the greed of princes and the usurpations of the Emperor. Within a few years twenty more cities joined the League, including the seven towns on the shores of Lake Constance. At the same time a League of Rhenish cities, from Mainz to Strassburg, was organised and in 1381 the two Leagues entered into a close alliance,

---

[1] Cf. the League of Six Cities in Upper Lusatia (Bautzen, Gorlitz, Labau, Loban, Kamenz and Zittau) formed in 1346 to protect trade routes from the west which passed through Meissen to Silesia, Bohemia and Poland.

Alarmed by the formidable character of the confederation and encouraged by Wenceslas, the territorial rulers framed a League of Princes in 1383. Their leaders were the Count of Wurtemburg and the Dukes of Bavaria. Leopold of Austria, who had succeeded to half the Habsburg inheritance in 1379, at first tried to play a neutral part by joining both Leagues. He was an able and ambitious ruler, and, reverting to earlier traditions of his house, was trying to piece together his territories on both sides of the Rhine.[1] Wenceslas sold him the Advocateship of Upper and Lower Suabia in 1381 and in 1382 he took advantage of local quarrels to assert suzerainty over the city of Bâle. As a result of these activities the Swiss became suspicious and prepared to support the movement against the princes in Germany.

As neither side was anxious for war, a temporary compromise was reached in the Alliance of Heidelberg in 1384. The cities agreed to join the princes in a great league of peace, but they refused to renounce their own associations and continued to maintain a hostile attitude. Duke Leopold became the chief object of their suspicion ; they resented both his Advocateship of Suabia and his membership of the League of Princes. Soon after the Alliance of Heidelburg they invited Bâle to join the League of Cities and entered into negotiations with the Swiss Confederation. Early in 1385 the Suabian League and the League of the Rhine concluded an offensive and defensive alliance, known as the Treaty of Constance, with Berne, Zurich, Zug and the imperial city of Soleure.[2] Leopold was thus confronted by a formidable confederation against him ; his position was made more difficult by a quarrel with

[1] Within four years Leopold had acquired the counties of Montford and Feldkirck, the lordship of Neuberg and the great estates of Count Rudolf of Hohenberg on the Upper Neckar.

[2] Lucerne joined indirectly by pledging herself to help Zurich ; the forest cantons held aloof for a time, as their local interests did not appear to be involved.

the Emperor, as a result of which Wenceslas took from him the Advocateship of Suabia and ordered the imperial cities to make war on him as a supporter of the Anti-Pope, Clement VII.

The capture of the little town of Rotenburg by Lucerne, (December, 1385), precipitated war with Leopold. At the summons of the Swiss, delegates of the Suabian League assembled at Ulm and prepared to carry out the agreements entered on at Constance. A message was sent to the League of the Rhine urging them to prepare for war and each city was called upon to supply its allotted number of pikes and mercenaries. It was believed that a general conflict with all the princes of southern Germany was on foot. The Swiss watchword—" Between the four forest cantons shall be a great Switzerland "—was borrowed and changed into—" Between the forests of the Vosges, Thuringia, Bohemia and the Lower Alps shall be a great union of free cities." Suddenly the enthusiasm for war seemed to evaporate and the German cities prepared to desert their allies. It was feared that war would ruin commerce ; the Rhenish cities were not interested in a war against the Habsburgs : Nuremburg hung back and the Suabian cities were conciliated by Leopold. The Leagues themselves were badly organised and alarmed supporters by their ineffective measures and vacillating policy. Finally, (February, 1386), eleven cities, including Strassburg and Bâle, signed a four months armistice with Leopold and before it had expired the Leagues had decided to render no help to Switzerland.

This desertion of their allies by the Leagues was a fatal blunder. The Swiss defeated Leopold without their aid and by the battle of Sempach, (1386), set the seal on their independence. Two years later the long-postponed war between the cities and the princes of southern Germany at last broke out. The Suabian cities were defeated at Döffingen by Count Eberhard of Wurtemburg, (August,

1388), and the League of the Rhine was routed at Worms by the Palsgrave, (November, 1388). Wenceslas turned against the cities and, in May, 1389, dissolved their Leagues as "contrary to God, the King, the Empire and the Law." [1] The Treaty known as The Peace of Eger, (1389), brought the war to an end, but at the expense of the federal movement between the cities. The princes were not yet strong enough to absorb the cities, but they were able to prevent them from achieving common political development. The collapse of the Suabian League and the League of the Rhine proved that the cities of the south and west were too near the headquarters of the great German houses and too much divided among themselves to solve the problem of independent survival.

3.   THE HANSEATIC LEAGUE

Unlike the cities of Upper Germany, the cities of the north at first found few obstacles in the way of federal union. A large measure of freedom followed from the *Drang nach Osten* policy of Habsburg and Luxemburg Emperors; in the later Middle Ages the north was neglected by the great princely houses and for a time lesser territorial families were not strong enough to endanger municipal independence. The great plain of Lower Germany, with its long rivers flowing into the North Sea and the Baltic, offered special opportunities for commercial development. Not only the over-land trade of the south, but the markets of England, the Netherlands, Scandinavia, Poland and Russia were accessible to the sea-faring merchants of the coast towns. The luxuries of the East and the products of Italy came from the south, and together with German commodities, were exchanged for the cloth and raw wool of England and the Netherlands, the timber and fish of Scandinavia and the wax, leather and furs of Russia.

[1] The League of the Seven Cities of Lake Constance alone survived.

On the Swedish island of Gotland, Wisby, a city of German merchants, was built ; in the thirteenth century it was connected with thirty cities, ranging from Reval to Cologne, and was the clearing house for the commerce of north-eastern Europe. *Navigare est necesse, vivere non est necesse* was the motto cut over the door of a guild house in Bremen and it is typical of the spirit in which the merchants of Lower Germany built up a great carrying trade between East and West.

The origin of the Hanseatic League may be traced to informal associations of north German merchants, which arose in the second half of the twelfth century for purposes of carrying on trade with Russia, monopolising the fishing grounds of the Baltic and buying the raw wool of England and the manufacturers' cloth of Flemish cities. Confederations of merchants guilds or Hansas were organised in connection with the great fair of Champagne ; more important than these was the Hansa of London, which had its centre at Bruges and consisted of a group of merchant guilds from seventeen cities associated together for regulation of commerce, especially in wool, with England.[1] At first these associations were not predominantly German, but the fall of Henry the Lion and the break-up of his duchy, (1180), caused the cities of the Baltic to become more independent and to draw together for purposes of trade. The first formal treaty of alliance was made between citizens of Lübeck and Hamburg in 1241 ; by it they bound themselves to unite in punishing all who interfered with their business and to pool expenses for common defence. In 1259 the merchants of Lübeck, Rostock and Wismar formed a League against highway-robbers and pirates, the terms of which ran as follows :—" We, the citizens of Lübeck, Rostock and Wismar . . . have in

[1] England was mainly an agricultural country and, partly owing to slow urban development, was still content to allow its export trade to depend on foreign enterprise. North Germany had a maritime commercial policy before England.

common council decreed . . . that all who rob merchants in churches, in cemeteries, on water or on land, shall be outlaws and punished by all cities and merchants. No matter where these robbers go with their booty, the city or land that receives them shall be held equally guilty . . . and shall be proscribed by all cities and merchants."

The success of these defensive alliances and the advantages of co-operation for the control of foreign markets soon made the practice popular. German merchants abroad bound themselves closely together in *Bundnisse* and *Genossenschaften*. The German merchants of Wisby were often referred to as *communes mercatores* ; they had their own seal bearing the inscription *sigillum Theutonicorum in Gotlandia manentium* [1] and that of merchants trading with them was inscribed *sigillum Theutonicorum Gotlandian frequentancium*.[2] German merchants enjoyed common privileges in England, in Flanders and in the S. Petershof of Novgorod at least from the thirteenth century. It is not surprising that they began to hold assemblies in Germany to discuss common interests. In 1299 representatives of the merchants of Westphalia and the cities of the Baltic met at Lübeck and in the following year commerce with Flanders was discussed at a meeting of merchants from the whole of Lower Germany and from Poland, Wisby and Riga. Treatment of the body of German merchants as a single unit is first clearly apparent in English records of the early fourteenth century when reference is made to the " Hansa of German merchants," (*hansa domus mercatorum Alemannie*). A little later similar expressions were used in Norway and in Novgorod.[3]

---

[1] Seal of the Germans dwelling in Gotland.

[2] Seal of the Germans frequenting Gotland.

[3] In Norway the expression *mercatores de hansa Theutonicorum* appears in 1343, 1348 and 1350. Cf. *Theutonicorum hansa* mercatores at Novgorod, *c.* 1350. *Vide* Dr. Walther Stein : Zur Entstehung und Bedeutung der Deutschen Hanse. *Hansische Geschichtsblätter*, 1911, pp. 265–365.

The Hanseatic League, in the full sense, did not come into being until the word *civitates* replaced the word *mercatores* and a community or league of cities was substituted for a community or league of merchants. Doctor Walther Stein has shown that this change took place in 1358 when a war with Flanders compelled the merchants, themselves patrician oligarchs, to identify the cities which they governed with the old *Hansa mercatorum Alemannie.* For the first time they used the expression " cities of the German Hansa." [1] In the following year " all cities belonging together to the Hansa of the Germans " [2] were summoned to send representatives to Lübeck to discuss the war with Flanders, navigation in the Sound and common action against pirates. The Hansa of merchants had become a Hansa of cities, but the substantial cause or *raison d'être* of unity remained economic and not political.

The strength of the League was shown by the success of its undertakings. Trade routes were patrolled and protected by land and sea. Courts of arbitration were set up to decide disputes between members and their sentences were enforced by threats of expulsion from the League. Assistance was provided to members to suppress democratic agitations and maintain a patrician government in power.[3] Treaties were arranged with foreign powers securing privileges for the League ; [4] if favourable conditions were refused, princes were coerced by threats of an economic boycott and attacks on merchant ships. It was inevitable that the wealth, monopolies and power of the League should rouse jealousy and opposition and

---

[1] Jenich stad van der Dudesolgen henze.

[2] Omnes communiter ad hansam Theutonicum pertinentes civitates.

[3] In 1417 the Diet of the League passed a law forbidding any member to allow its citizens to elect the *Rat.*

[4] In England the Hansards were treated as the " most favoured nation," e.g. the tariff they paid on imported cloth was less by almost two-thirds than that paid by other alien merchants and they had also the privilege of selling certain commodities retail.

bring about a series of wars with the Baltic powers as bitter as the conflicts between Venice and Genoa.

In the fourteenth century Denmark was the chief power in Scandinavia and her king was the protagonist in war against the League. Danish influence had once been paramount along the southern shores of the Baltic, but the rise of German cities and internal dissensions had brought about the decay of Danish commerce and the control of the exits from the Baltic by the League. The issue was complicated by the movements of herring shoals, which drew after them the fishers and traders of the north. Until the thirteenth century the herring visited the coast of Pomerellen and west Prussia every year and trade in fish was the basis of the commerce of Lübeck, Wismar, Stralsund and Danzic. Then the fish changed their habits and abandoned the southern shores of the Baltic for the coasts of Scania and Norway. Fishers and traders followed and, after a series of petty engagements with sailors from England, Scotland, Holland and Scandinavia, the Hansa merchants destroyed a number of trading posts and established themselves on the coast of Scania in depots fortified by trenches and palisades. An attempt to recover control and revive Danish commerce was begun by Waldemar III, King of Denmark, (1340–1374). He demanded toll from all ships passing through the Sound and, by seizing Scania from Sweden, threatened the League's control of the herring fisheries. War broke out in 1361, Waldemar led a fleet and an army against Wisby and, as the inhabitants foolishly met him in open battle instead of standing a siege,[1] the city was captured, sacked and reduced to a heap of ruins. The Danes gained full control of the Baltic straits and used it to exact heavy tolls and plunder German shipping. After some desultory fighting the League was roused to vigorous action. Alliances were made with

[1] Wisby was surrounded by walls two miles in circumference defended by forty towers.

Sweden, Mecklenburg, Holstein and Schleswig. A great council of war was held at Cologne, (November, 1367), attended by representatives of the territorial allies, ten cities of the League and Amsterdam and Brieg.[1] A fleet was raised from members of the League, of which the Baltic cities contributed by far the greater number. A *Pfundzoll* or tax of four English pennies was imposed on every pound of Hanseatic merchandise. In the spring of 1368 the ships of the North Sea joined forces with those of the Baltic and captured and destroyed, not only nearly all the fortresses on the coast of Scania, but Copenhagen itself. Waldemar was forced to make peace. In 1370 the Treaty of Stralsund was signed, which gave the League control of the fisheries of the Sound, and full rights over all toll and customs collected there. It also acquired all castles and strongholds on the coast of Scania for a term of fifteen years and the extraordinary guarantee that no king should be crowned in Denmark until he had been accepted by the League and had confirmed its privileges. The Treaty of Stralsund shows the League at the height of its power ; it had secured complete control of commerce in the Baltic and a voice in the internal affairs of its most dangerous rival, Denmark.

Apart from its economic policy, there is little to say about the constitution and administration of the League, because it showed itself remarkably sterile in institutional development. It had no permanent officials, no army, no permanent navy, no treasury and no executive. There was not even the normal sign of a corporate organisation, a common seal, though the double eagle of Lübeck was used as such, especially abroad. The administration of the League

[1] The cities of the League which were represented were Lübeck, Rostock, Wismar, Stralsund, Thorn, Elbing, Kampen, Hardewich, and Elborg. It is often said that 77 Hansa cities sent representatives to the Confederation of Cologne, but this statement is incorrect. At Cologne it was decided to invite the co-operation of other cities and thirty-one are said to have accepted.

was divided up among its members and was entirely
dependent on the co-operation and energy of *Ratsherren*
of particular cities. Even the judicial courts of arbitration were under local control. Almost the only positive
sign of *Bundesorgane* were the sessions of Hansa Diets,
either general or provincial, which met at irregular intervals.
These Diets were attended by *Ratsendeboten* or representatives of the Patrician governing bodies of the constituent
members : only sworn *Ratmänner* were allowed to take
part in deliberations. The expense and long journey
to the place of session—usually Lübeck—was regarded
as a heavy burden. In 1430 Prussian members were
granted the privilege of being represented by only two
Ratsendeboten ; from 1450 onwards the League tried to
compel attendance by fines and threats of expulsion. It
had been decided in 1430 that, except in special circumstances, Hansa Diets should meet every three years, but
it was found impossible to carry out this policy. From
1400 onwards general interest in the business of the League
declined and the effect can be seen in the number of sessions
of the Hansa Diet. Forty-three general sessions are
recorded ; of these twenty-four took place between 1363
and 1400, twelve between 1400 and 1440 and seven between
1440 and 1480. Summons to Hansa Diets stated the business of the session, which provincial diets were supposed
to discuss before the general assembly took place. The
loose organisation of the League, the jealousy of its members
and the great distances between them must have made
preparation of the agenda very difficult.[1] The task was
usually undertaken by Lübeck, but her authority was
very much resented by other cities. When the Hansa
Diet assembled economic policy and foreign relations
were discussed and decrees were passed. We do not know
any details about its procedure, as information comes
mainly from the *Rezesse* or registers of legislation and

[1] Prussian cities demanded three months' notice.

compacts which were written down before the *Rezess* (recess) of the assembly.[1] From numerous disputes on the subject we know that the decision of the majority bound, not only the minority present and voting, but also absent members. In all general sessions Lübeck *hält das Wort*, that is, acted as speaker or President. Lübeck, in fact, acted as a sort of informal executive to the Hansa Diet; her *Ratsherren* issued summons, drafted agenda, initiated much of the legislation, supervised the enforcement of statutes, heard complaints and conducted the bulk of official correspondence with outside powers. In spite of opposition from Cologne and other members, the League was virtually controlled by Lübeck and the neighbouring Wendish cities. Though the Hansa Diet was an instrument of government with great potentialities, the oligarchic tendency of the cities reasserted itself in their federal organisation, and was an effective check to the evolutions of institutions.

Difficulties in the way of estimating the geographical extent of the League at any given time are immense. Numerous fifteenth and sixteenth century lists of members are extant, but they are not official and do not agree with each other. The longest lists enumerate about seventy cities, a number which appears often in the history of the League. In Russia reference was frequently made to the " Seventy Cities "; chroniclers often state the number as seventy-seven, but modern historians are agreed that this number was a mere *Zahlenspielerei*, meaning an indefinitely large number. The largest Hansa Diet was probably that of 1447, which was attended by representatives of thirty-eight cities. To contemporaries, the test of membership was probably the right of sharing in the

---

[1] Lübeck began to preserve *Rezesse* in 1361, Wismar and Stralsund in 1363, Hamburg in 1369 and Danzic in 1375. The Diet of the Swiss Confederation preserved its records (*Abschiede*) in the same way.

foreign privileges of the Hansa. Not only was the right frequently granted and withdrawn, but it was held by cities whose names appear on no list and whose representatives were not summoned to Diets; it was also held by persons dwelling in the country or even by villages. The inhabitants of Prussia seem to have had a general qualification for membership and many small places in Westphalia, where domestic industry flourished, had certain rights. It is, in fact, impossible to draw a clear dividing line between small places which did and did not belong to the League; probably such a line never was drawn or was altered so often that it had little significance. Certainly the total number of Hansa cities fluctuated, perhaps never remaining constant for as long as a decade. Doctor Stein has enumerated a total of one hundred and sixty-four cities whose membership was temporary or permanent, either certainly or probably.[1] This total does not include foreign cities, like Narva and Dinant, which enjoyed a full share in Hansa rights, or the cities of Poland which were half members of the League. The number one hundred and sixty-four, it must be emphasised, does not represent actual conditions at any given time. The evidence, on the whole, suggests that the circle of Hansa cities grew wider between the middle of the fourteenth and the middle of the fifteenth century and that the number of members was greatest between 1430 and 1470.

Hansa cities were scattered over a wide territorial area.

---

[1] The total figure is arrived at as follows:

Cities of the Rhineland and the Netherlands	.	29
Cities of Westphalia and Lower Saxony .	.	76 (48 + 28)
Cities of the Brandenburg Mark .	.	14
Cities of Holstein and Mecklenburg .	.	24
Prussian Cities	.	6
Cities of Silesia and Poland (Breslau and Cracow)		2
Livonian Cities	.	11
Northern cities (Wisby and Stockholm) .	.	2

Total . 164

In 1347 they were divided into thirds, each of which was further subdivided into two. The Rhineland and Westphalia and Prussia made up one third, Lower Saxony and the Wendish and Pomeranian cities another, and Gottland and Livonia the last. The fulcrum of the League was found in the Wendish cities acting in co-operation with their Pomeranian neighbours. Lübeck was the capital of the Wendish area and, in that province, Stralsund and Rostock stood next to her at first, though Hamburg, from her position on the Elbe, gradually came to claim the second place. Brunswick and Magdeburg were the chief cities of the Saxon area, closely followed by Goslar and Hildesheim ; Bremen on the Weser was the most important city on the coast. In Prussia, Danzic and Riga and in Westphalia, Dortmund, Soest and Munster held the first place. Cologne was the capital of the Rhineland and Kampen was the only important member in the Netherlands.[1] Thus the area under the influence of the League stretched right across the great plain of Northern Europe, cutting across territorial and even national frontiers and blocked only by the backward civilisation of Slavonic lands.

Even by the end of the fourteenth century causes had begun to operate which brought about the decline and fall of the Hanseatic League. The most important political changes which had a direct effect upon it were the Union of Kalmar and the Slav revival in the north-east. The Union of Kalmar was fatal to Hanseatic control of the Baltic straits. In 1397 Margaret, daughter of Waldemar, and Queen of Norway, Sweden and Denmark, attempted to unite the three kingdoms permanently by a formal act of union, ratified by the Council of each country. Though Sweden broke away again half a century later, the concerted action of the Scandinavian powers was enough to

---

[1] Halle, Breslau and Cracow were isolated, though important from their position on trade routes.

destroy the Hanseatic monopoly in the Baltic Sea. Almost simultaneously the union of Poland and Lithuania, (1386), brought to an end the Hanseatic monopoly of trade in the north-east. Direct intercourse with the great markets of Kieff and Novgorod was blocked by Polish hostility and by war in Prussia. When the Teutonic Knights were forced to cede West Prussia to Poland by the Treaty of Thorn, (1466), the great cities of the Vistula abandoned the League and German overland communications with the northern plain were seriously endangered.

The heavy losses within the Baltic were rendered more harmful by other changes of a definitely economic kind. The fishing interests of the League were severely damaged by a second migration of the herring shoals. About 1425 the herrings ceased to visit the coast of Scania, but remained in the North Sea, choosing the coast of Holland as their summer resort. Thus the privileges and fortresses for which the League had contended in the fourteenth century became almost valueless. Amsterdam was built on herrings in the fifteenth century, just as the Baltic cities had been at an earlier time. The rise of new maritime powers threatened German commerce in other directions. Merchants and sailors of England and Holland began to challenge the Hansa monopoly. In the fifteenth century opposition came chiefly from Zeeland and Holland ; the Dutch began to build larger and more seaworthy vessels and to claim a share in the distribution of both raw materials and manufactured goods. Their geographical position made it natural for them to become freight-carriers as well as fishermen, and in so doing they were forced into open conflict with the League. In 1415 the Hansa Diet passed a decree forbidding the entry into the Baltic of any goods which had not been purchased in a Hansa town. The Dutch resented the regulations and allied themselves with the Danes against the League. Inter-mittent naval war followed in which the Dutch were on the whole successful. By 1510 the carrying trade of the League had passed to the merchantmen of Holland and Zeeland. Still graver economic losses were caused by changes in the highways of commerce. The discovery of the Cape route to India destroyed overland trade from the east and south. Troubles in Russia were equally destructive of trade in the north-east ; Ivan III expelled German merchants from Novgorod in 1478 and the city ceased to be a Hansa counter in 1494. The efforts of the Portuguese and Spaniards to discover new markets and new trade routes led to the exploration of Africa and the discovery of America, and their success shifted the whole balance of European trade. The main stream of commerce ceased to flow across Germany from the south-east and the harbours of the Mediterranean gave way to the ports of the Atlantic. The geographical situation of the Hansa cities made it difficult for them to take advantage of the change ; they ceased to be distributors of commodities from the east just at the time when the Atlantic powers were struggling for the monopoly of the markets of Africa and the Americas.

More serious than all these external causes of decline were the narrow policy and the defective constitutional structure of the League itself. If it had been organised on a broader and less eclectic basis, it ought to have survived the strain of great political and economic changes and have been ready to take advantage of the Revolt of the Netherlands and thus recover its carrying trade from the Dutch. The institutional development of the League had been insufficient ; its informal origin and the absence of common danger from any one territorial power had concealed the necessity for structural reform. There was no adequate financial system and no strong administration. The Hansa Diets did not represent the common interest and distant members considered that they had no effective control of policy. The decline in the number

13

of Diets, the difficulty of enforcing attendance, the fierce contests for precedence [1] and resistance to majority decisions were significant of fatal internal weakness. The League lacked a genuine national basis. Even the Baltic wars did not affect all members closely enough to create a strong government. The cities of the Rhine, the Weser and the Elbe had an outlet on the North Sea and had only a secondary interest in Scandinavian policy; the cities of Upper Germany strove to divert overland trade from the north in order to secure a monopoly of profit; the cities of Prussia were anxious to play their own hand in the eastern Baltic and were ready to desert the League when Poland acquired the Vistula basin. The Wendish oligarchy was not strong enough to coerce recalcitrants.

From the outset the territorial situation was fraught with difficulty and danger. The cities were dependent on rural districts for the food they ate or exported, yet they had no authority over it. No attempt was made to include even those villages and open districts which enjoyed Hansa rights. The army of the League consisted of enlisted mercenaries. When the necessity arose treaties and pacts were made with neighbouring princes, who undertook to hire out their soldiers to the League. Troops of this kind were most unsatisfactory and consequently were used as little as possible. The effect of military weakness can be seen in several different directions. Colonisation was virtually impossible and the commerce of the League was dependent on the fortunes and favours of foreign powers.[2] Only economic weapons could be used against powers like Poland and Russia. The loss of Cracow, Breslau and the cities of Prussia showed that diplomacy and business relations could not permanently

[1] Lübeck's presidency was challenged by Cologne: Bremen and Hamburg disputed for the third place: in 1399 the Prussian cities claimed to rank after Lübeck and Stralsund.

[2] For example, ships were of no value in keeping open commerce with Novgorod and the Russian plain.

compete against foreign armies. In Germany itself the lack of an army rendered an effective resistance to territorial aggression impossible. The dangers of the situation were even graver than in Upper Germany, as only four imperial cities [1] were members of the League. The remainder were at least nominally subject to local territorial rulers and as soon as the policy of consolidating principalities was begun they were in constant danger of absorption. The League refused to face the issue, adopted the policy of never interfering in quarrels between cities and their superiors and boasted that it had never undertaken a German war. As the League shrank from the difficult task of the unification of Lower Germany, the duty fell to the princes, who in the long run showed themselves capable of founding the strong and organic system of government which the country required. We can see the beginning of change in the Mark of Brandenburg. The Elector Frederick II engaged in a vehement quarrel about judicial supremacy with the citizens of Berlin-Kölln ; in 1442 he appointed a *Rat* of his own nominees, cancelled civic privileges and prohibited all leagues with other cities. The other cities of the Mark soon withdrew from the League ; in 1498 only Stendal and Salzwedel were members and twenty years later they also had resigned. The withdrawal of the cities of Brandenburg was the first important secession of cities on German soil. It was followed by the loss of Halle, Halberstadt and lesser Saxon cities and, taken together with the rapid decline of Hansa power in the East, marks the end of the territorial influence of the League.

When we come to analyse the structure of the Hanseatic League we find in it no true federal characteristics. Its members did not enjoy complete independence in those matters which concerned them collectively. The League never achieved organic unity and thus lacked the essential

[1] Cologne, Lübeck, Dortmund and Goslar.

characteristic of a body politic. Divorced from the life and interests of rural districts, it avoided national responsibility. The League itself was the triumph of oligarchy ; it was the work of patrician merchants in a number of cities who agreed to co-operate for purposes of protecting and extending their business activities. The result shows that undisciplined self-interest in any one section of a community may be as dangerous to its health as the overgrowth of certain tissues in the human body. In the acquisition of wealth, in the development of commerce and in the search for and exploitation of markets the ruling oligarchs showed marvellous energy and power of organisation, but their political horizon was always limited by short views of profit and loss. They neglected industry, crushed the craft guilds and the proletariate and maintained their position of privilege by ruthless economic boycott. As they had ignored the interests of the German peasant and alienated the mass of their fellow-citizens, they had nothing to offer but commercial prosperity and nothing to lose except their wealth. When political changes and a new commercial orientation injured economic prosperity they found that they had laid their foundations of power on shifting sand. Though a great sea-power, they had no colonial policy ; though they believed in strong government in individual cities, they had shirked the task of creating a general Executive ; though they depended for life and safety on the foodstuffs and man-power of the country, they had ignored the territorial problem on the solution of which the future of Germany depended. By avoiding positive political action and by concentrating on material prosperity, the Hanseatic League showed the truth of the proposition that the state cannot live by economic policy alone.

CHAPTER VIII

THE SWISS CONFEDERATION OF CITIES AND CANTONS [1]

HISTORICAL SURVEY. THE FEDERAL STRUCTURE.

1. HISTORICAL SURVEY

TO understand the rise of the Swiss Confederation it is necessary to remember that Habsburg territorial policy was not confined to the eastern borders of the Empire, but that the family regarded their hereditary estates in the valleys of the Aar and the Reuss, in Alsace and in the Black Forest as so many jumping-off places for the control of Upper Germany. Their object was to acquire the whole of the ancient duchy of Suabia and as much as possible of the fallen kingdom of Burgundy. Working with the patient tenacity of ants, they slowly pieced together scraps of territory in southern Suabia and Lower Alsace. They recognised the importance of control of the Alpine passes, at first mainly for commercial reasons, and became more and more intent on asserting their authority over the Alpine population. Their policy was resisted by the cities and rural communities of the district, who gradually drew together to resist what they believed to be unwarrantable aggression. In this way the first Swiss Confederation was formed ; it was in origin a union of a small part of southern

[1] The material for this chapter is almost entirely derived from *Histoire de la Confédération Suisse* by J. Dierauer, translated by A. Reymond, (Vols. I and II, Lausanne, 1911 and 1912).

Suabia, organised to combat the land-hunger of the Habsburgs.

The failure of the Habsburgs to overcome resistance was due primarily to the geography of the district. Western Switzerland—Switzerland west of the S. Gotthard pass —consists of a plain district in the north and two enormous ranges of mountains, divided by the deep trench of the Rhone Valley in the south. These ranges or series of ranges are the Bernese Oberland and the Pennine Alps, which together form two great walls flanked on the west by Mount Blanc and the Diablerets. These walls are not parallel, as they converge in the district where there is a knot of mountain ridges, in the neighbourhood of the Rhone glacier. There the Rhine, the Inn, the Ticino, the Rhone and the Reuss all have their source. To the east lies the confused mass of the mountains of the Grisons and the Tyrol. The natural centre of Swiss history lies within the badly drawn triangle formed by the Aar and the Reuss. The head waters of the Reuss are in the canton of Uri near the top of the S. Gotthard pass ; the river flows through Uri into Lake Lucerne, which lies between the canton of Schwyz and that of Unterwalden ; it then runs in a north-westerly direction along the frontier of the canton of Zurich and joins the Aar just south of Hawks Castle or Habsburg. The Aar rises near the Rhone glacier, flows north-west through Berne to a point north of Lake Neuchâtel and then runs north-east to its confluence with the Reuss. The united rivers flow into the Rhine above Bâle on the edge of the Black Forest. The triangle of the Aar and the Reuss represents the original Swiss Confederation. The forest cantons lie in the basin of the Reuss ; Lucerne and Berne lie on the Reuss and the Aar respectively and the territory of Zurich is bounded by the Reuss on the west. Each city owed its importance primarily to geographical situation. Lucerne and Zurich were built where rivers emerge from lakes and were provided with easy communications north to the Rhine and south over the S. Gotthard pass to Italy. Berne also enjoyed easy communications with the Rhine and had the military advantage of a situation on a peninsula of sandstone rock, with the Aar flowing more than half way round it, a hundred feet below.

Resistance to outside control began in the forest cantons of Uri, Schwyz and Unterwalden and was provoked by agents sent to collect taxes for or to exercise jurisdiction in the name of Rudolf of Habsburg.[1] The first record of the league between them is the Pact of 1290. Its introductory paragraph runs as follows : " It is a good thing for public utility if communities agree to preserve peace and order. Therefore, let all know that the men of the Valley of Uri and the commune of those who live within the mountains, considering the dangers that threaten them, and in order to be better able to defend themselves and their possessions, have, in good faith, promised mutually to assist each other with aid, counsel and support, with their persons as well as with their possessions . . . against each and all who may try to molest, harm or injure any of them in their persons or in their possessions. . . ." The cantons who formed this league were all inhabited by a German-speaking population, technically subjects of the Emperor. The peasants of Uri were nearly all serfs, bound to perform certain fixed duties for imperial officers ; the peasants of Unterwalden were mainly serfs and those of Schwyz freemen. For this reason the men of Schwyz took the lead and finally gave their name to the whole confederation. The alliance was at first purely defensive and was directed against the exercise of arbitrary power by Habsburg bailiffs.

When Rudolf died in 1291 the three forest cantons entered into a perpetual alliance binding themselves to offer

[1] The Habsburgs were Counts of Zurich and claimed lordship over the upper basins of the Reuss and the Aar.

resistance to all outside interference and to secure a native-born magistracy and customary procedure in their courts of law. The alliance was tantamount to a claim to complete autonomy, thinly disguised by the conservative style of its articles. The three cantons were determined to turn the prevalent territorialism to their own advantage, instead of allowing themselves to be victimised by it. The means adopted to achieve this end were characteristic of the legalism and violence of the time ; they sought from the Emperor recognition of their status as feudal units or immediate vassals and thus hoped to secure a legal basis for armed resistance to the claims of the Habsburg house. This design was made practicable by the failure of Habsburg imperial ambitions after the death of Rudolf. Adolf of Nassau, (1297), granted to Schwyz and Uri letters of franchise confirming declarations of immediacy or tenancy in chief made by Frederick II. In 1309 Henry VII issued a confirmation of these letters and also gave to the men of Unterwalden a charter confirming in general terms the liberties and rights which they claimed to have received from his predecessors. The arrival of an imperial bailiff to exercise judicial and military authority over the three cantons was welcomed as clear proof of their direct relation to the Emperor. As long as the Habsburgs were excluded from the imperial throne, the way of safety for the confederates lay in dependence on the Emperor. When the double imperial election occurred in 1314 the three cantons prepared to support Lewis of Bavaria against the Habsburg candidate, Frederick of Austria. Their adhesion to the Wittelsbach cause made the outbreak of war inevitable.

The men of the Cantons had certain advantages over the armies of the Habsburgs. The nature of their country made it easy to defend and difficult to attack. During the thirteenth century mercenary levies had been raised from time to time in the cantons and on their return had given the peasants some knowledge of the art of war.

They had introduced the use of a heavy halbert, wielded rather like the English quarter-staff and effective in unhorsing mounted troops. Leopold of Habsburg was ignorant of the country and of the hardiness and valour of his opponents. He collected a considerable force, representing the feudal levies of nearly all the chief families of north-west Switzerland, and laid his plans for a double invasion of the cantons. Otto of Strassburg, bailiff of Habsburg lands in Burgundy, was to attack Unterwalden, crossing from the Bernese Oberland by the Brünig pass, while Leopold himself led an army from Zug into Schwyz by the defile of Lake Aegeri. Leopold neglected the obvious precaution of reconnaissance and allowed his troops to be entrapped near the village of Morgarten, on the narrow track between the southern end of the lake and the overhanging mountain side, (November, 1315). The peasants rolled down stones and tree trunks from the high ground. The Habsburg army was caught as by an avalanche, thrown into great confusion and easily routed by a furious charge of the men of Schwyz, armed with their halberts. Leopold and those of his followers who escaped a merciless slaughter fled in disorder and when Otto of Strassburg heard the news he withdrew his forces with all speed from Unterwalden. Thus the first victory of the confederates was due primarily to the ignorance of the enemy and to the choice of ground for battle on which cavalry could not be used to advantage.

The victory of Morgarten encouraged the cantons to form a new league, which, though formally acknowledging imperial authority, denied it as far as autonomy was concerned. Lucerne, the first city to become a member, joined the Confederation in 1332. Zurich, under the direction of Rudolf Brun, concluded a perpetual alliance with Lucerne and the three forest cantons in 1351. The signatories not only bound themselves in a league for mutual protection, but guaranteed local autonomy, defined the limits of the jurisdiction of the Confederation and provided for courts of arbitration and a Diet for discussion of common business. The treaty with Zurich became the model for all federal alliances and was the basis of public law in Switzerland until 1848. The rural cantons of Glarus, (east of Schwyz), and Zug, (between Schwyz and Zurich), entered the Confederation in 1352. Berne, the chief city on the upper Aar with a long tradition of federal alliances with the towns, cantons and seigneuries of the west behind it, joined the Confederation in 1353. Her accession completed the roll of the eight *alten Orte* or original cantons of the Confederation. The territory of members then included the whole central area of the Alpine district, stretching, west to east, from Lake Neuchâtel to Lake Zurich and, north to south, from the Rhine Falls at Schaffhausen to the head of the S. Gotthard pass. All the members were German by birth and speech ; in the critical century of formation the Confederacy had a unity of race and language which has since been lost.

The Habsburgs did not abandon their rights over the cantons without a prolonged struggle. After Morgarten the danger either from peaceful penetration or from armies of invasion was continual. Leopold of Austria brought matters to a head in 1386, when, in pursuance of the family policy of Suabian annexation,[1] he led an expedition from Baden into the canton of Lucerne. He encountered the forces of the Confederation at Sempach and, after some savage fighting in which the superiority of halbert-men over cavalry was once more proved, the Habsburg army was routed and Leopold himself was slain on the field. Two years later, (1388), Leopold's son was defeated, in spite of overwhelming numerical superiority, by the army of Glarus at Näfels. These victories set a seal on independence of Habsburg rule. They were the direct result of military efficiency, developed by hard

[1] Vide Chapter vii, § 2.

training, local organisation and the use of infantry.[1]
The soldiers of the Confederation were organised in districts
under the banners of towns, guilds or villages. The
rural cantons elected their own officers, the *Stadträte* of
urban communities appointed captains. Co-operation
between local units was so well ordered that an army of
twenty thousand men could be raised in a few days and,
owing to the absence of heavy armour, could be led to a
given point with remarkable speed. In the field the local
contingents combined to form a moving column, which
hurled itself against the ranks of the enemy in a series of
rapid but regular attacks. Sir Charles Oman writes:
" A Swiss army was simple in its elements and easy to
handle." The adoption of column tactics made elaborate
manœuvres unnecessary. For this reason there were no
great Swiss generals and small danger of military interference in politics.

After Sempach and Näfels the Habsburg ceased to be
a serious menace and for over a century the Swiss were
content to remain part of the Empire. The imperial immediacy they had received seemed a sufficient guarantee of
independence. In the fifteenth century they continued to
extend their frontiers, resisting and helping to destroy
the new middle kingdom of Burgundy. When the period
of intercalary or non-Habsburg Emperors came to an end
their immediacy lost its value. Maximilian tried to use
the occasion of the Suabian war to reassert the authority
of his house in Switzerland, but his armies were repeatedly
defeated in the field and he was forced to sign the treaty
of Bâle, (1499), by which he renounced all rights of suzerainty over the confederates and their allies. The renunciation was tantamount to a separation of the Confederation

[1] Vide *Art of War in the Middle Ages* by Sir Charles Oman (New
Edition, Vol. II, Book XI).

The halbert was replaced by an eighteen-foot pike with ten inches
of steel; later, pike-men were supported by light infantry armed
with hand guns.

from the Empire. The essentials were secured in 1499, but the full sovereignty of the Confederation was not explicitly recognised until the Peace of Westphalia in 1648.

2. THE FEDERAL STRUCTURE

Like the English Constitution, the Constitution of the Confederation was unwritten, that is, it rested, not on comprehensive statutes, but on custom and judicial decisions. There were, however, certain legal agreements of the same order of constitutional importance as the English Charters of Liberty, Petition of Right and Bill of Rights : of these the most significant were the Priests' Charter, the Convention of Sempach and the Convention of Stanz. A brief examination of these federal acts is necessary to an understanding of the federal structure.

In 1370 the cantons of Uri, Schwyz, Unterwalden, Zurich, Lucerne and Zug concluded an agreement known as the Priests' Charter, (*Pfaffenbrief*), for the purpose of safeguarding public peace and the rights of native tribunals, which at the time were threatened by Habsburg and ecclesiastical intrigue. Everyone dwelling in the territory of the Confederation was forced to take an oath of loyalty to it. Ecclesiastics were denied the right to summon subjects of the Confederation before any foreign judge or to cite them to appear in an ecclesiastical court except for matrimonial or testamentary causes. The penalties for breach of the law were social boycott, and the withdrawal of protection. Laymen were forbidden to appeal to ecclesiastical courts except in ecclesiastical causes. No armed expedition was permitted unless it was organised by lawful public authority ; the forces of the Confederation were to be utilised to punish offenders and exact indemnities. Finally, the Confederates undertook to punish all disturbers of the peace and to police the highways from Zurich to the *stibende Brug*, (foaming bridge), of S. Gotthard. The interest of this concordat lies not so much in the limits set to ecclesiastical jurisdiction, as in the agreement to undertake common measures for the internal welfare of the confederates. Hitherto the federal organisation had been used only for purposes of attack and defence against foreign enemies. The prohibition of private war, the suppression of robbery and disorder and the compulsory oath of allegiance were signs of the beginning of internal unity, the natural preparation for the formation of an organic society.

The Convention of Sempach, (1393), which included all members who had taken part in the recent war with Austria, carried the new policy one stage further. The Priests' Charter was confirmed and a series of regulations for the maintenance of military discipline were laid down. No soldiers, even the wounded, were to leave the field before the end of the battle. Military crimes were to be severely punished by the judges of the districts to which offenders belonged. Pillage, except by permission of the captains, was prohibited ; all plunder must be handed over to the captains and shared out equally by them among the combatants. Assaults on women, sacrilege and attacks on ecclesiastical property were absolutely forbidden. These rules were the basis of the military law of the Confederation ; their constitutional importance lies in the common bargain to enforce them.

The Convention of Stanz, (1481), was the outcome of grave internal disorders which threatened to destroy the Confederation. Since the middle of the fourteenth century it had been clear that in certain directions the policy of the forest cantons ran counter to that of the cities. The strength of the Confederation consisted mainly in the union of opposites, a combination of the military forces and food supply of the country with the markets and superior knowledge of the towns. It was, however, inevitable that friction between the two groups of allies should

arise. The forest cantons, as the founders of the Confederation, maintained their position of leadership with obstinate
pride and often distrusted or repudiated the policy of the
cities, based on a wider knowledge of affairs.[1]   There was
also a sharp contrast between the primitive democracy
of the rural cantons and the oligarchy which, in fact, if
not always in theory, governed the cities.   Country
people feared that extension of urban influences would
be followed by loss of liberty.   A common cause of discord
was the rule of subject areas.   In the fourteenth century
disputes broke out over the Wäggi Tal,[2] which was at the
same time a dependent ally of Schwyz and under the
suzerainty of Lucerne.   More serious conflicts arose at
the beginning of the fifteenth century in connection with
the status and powers of the town of Zug.   When the
canton was finally emancipated from Habsburg authority,
(c. 1365), its country districts came under the jurisdiction
of the *amman* of Schwyz.   As the town of Zug developed,
friction between its law officers and those of the country
was common and was still further increased when the
Emperor Wenceslas granted full criminal jurisdiction to
the three rural communities of Zug, (1400).   An open
breach occurred in 1404 when the rural communities
demanded that the seal and archives of the canton should
be preserved by them instead of by the town.   The
government of Schwyz supported the claim and prepared
to send troops to capture and coerce the town.   The four
cantons of Lucerne, Zurich, Uri and Unterwalden took the
part of the urban community and for a time civil war and
even the dissolution of the Confederacy seemed inevitable.
Fortunately, war was averted by the disinterested arbitra-

[1] For example, in 1385, the forest cantons refused to join the
Suabian League, as their own interests did not appear to be directly
involved.
[2] On the left bank of Lake Zurich, north of the canton of Schwyz.
In the fifteenth century Schwyz and Zurich had many disputes over
frontier questions.

tion of Berne, Glarus and Soleure and the matter was referred to the Diet of the Confederation. In 1405, by order of the Diet, fines were imposed on Schwyz and the rural communities of Zug ; the town retained her custody of the seal and archives. The whole affair demonstrated the dangerous hostility between town and country, though it also showed the value of federal organisation as an agency of peace.

At the close of the Burgundian war, (1476), general resentment of the leadership taken by the cities of Lucerne, Zurich and Berne came to a head. The strong executives developed by the cities were actually much better suited to the direction of affairs than the democratic assemblies of the rural cantons. After the defeat of Charles the Bold the cities, became impatient with the federal machinery, which seemed unable to formulate and maintain a uniform policy in home and foreign affairs. Another cause of discontent was the misconduct and excesses of Swiss soldiers, which the rural cantons were unable to check. As the rural cantons showed themselves jealous and obstructive, urban members drew away from them and in 1477 Lucerne, Zurich and Berne signed at S. Urbain a treaty of perpetual alliance.[1] The legal right of Lucerne to enter into an alliance of the kind was doubtful, as she was bound by the pact of 1332 not to enter into any new league without the consent of the three forest cantons. It seemed as if the Confederation would split over what was apparently a point of law, but which actually was the result of the alignment of the three urban and five rural cantons in two hostile formations. Again the situation was saved by the intervention of the Diet and, after long and angry debates, the members realised the danger of schism [2] and came

[1] Friburg and Soleure were also signatories. The rural cantons had refused to admit them to membership of the Confederation.
[2] The work of pacification was undertaken by a hermit, Nicholas of Flüe, who was revered as a saint.

to the agreement known as the Convention of Stanz, (1481).

By the Convention of Stanz the Priests' Charter and the Convention of Sempach were confirmed and the several members agreed to maintain peace, avert civil war, and suppress by joint action all rebellion. The cities of Friburg and Soleure were admitted to membership of the Confederation, thus securing an equal number of urban and rural members. Further regulations were made about the equal division of the spoils of war. Each canton bound itself to punish evil-doers and prevent breaches of the peace within its boundaries. All levies dangerous to the common welfare and all unauthorised political assemblies were prohibited. The perilous consequences of disruption were so clearly recognised that even the rural cantons agreed to this limitation of political liberty. Finally, the Treaty bound, not only the ten confederates, but all who were in alliance with any one of them. The Convention of Stanz was an act of reunion after discord, an achievement in statecraft of the first order. Apart from the importance of particular clauses, its value lay in the triumph of centripetal over centrifugal forces and in the general recognition that both urban and rural communities must make sacrifices for the sake of the organic unity of the federal body.

By the beginning of the sixteenth century the Confederation had become something very different from the simple league of a small group of neighbouring cantons that it had been in the fourteenth century. It was composed of heterogenous elements, unequal in rights and duties and bound together by a bewildering tangle of alliances and acts of submission. In the first place stood the thirteen *Orte* or cantons enjoying full and exclusive rights of membership.[1] Second to them were the *Zugewandte*

---

[1] Bâle, Schaffhausen and Appenzell were admitted to the Confederation in 1501 : the circle of the confederates remained closed from that time until 1798.

Orte or allied cantons which received the protection of the Confederacy in return for military support. They were in possession of full local autonomy, but had no right to sit in the Federal Diet and no control over its decisions. The federated cantons of Valais and of the Grisons, the towns of Bienne, St. Gall, Rottweil and Mulhouse, the abbey of S. Gall and the county of Neuchâtel were the most important members of this class. In the last place stood the subject territories, bought or conquered by the Confederation or its members. The constitutional status of these areas was extremely varied. Some were governed by particular cantons, some by a group and some by the whole Confederation. They were not admitted to a share in the rights and liberties of the Confederation, but continued to be governed in much the same way as they had been by their former territorial rulers. Civil liberty in the form of local custom was guaranteed, but political liberty was denied.

The only federal organ capable of acting for the Confederation as a whole was the Diet. By it war was declared, peace negotiated, ambassadors received and despatched and treaties concluded. Like the Hansa Diet, it was composed of *Boten* or delegates from the several members. It met by reason of the decision of a previous Diet or at the request of any member of the Confederation. The result of its decision depended, normally, on the instructions given to delegates by cantonal authorities. It was and continued to be a congress of sovereign states, members of which reserved the right of rejecting a majority decision. The majority could not bind the minority, at least not so far as to compel military support.[1] The composition and procedure of the assembly were ill-ordered. Reports of debates were rarely compiled and we are dependent for our knowledge of proceedings on the summaries of business

[1] As late as 1515 a proposal to force the minority to accept the decision of the majority was rejected by the Diet.

14

compiled by the local Chancellor and handed over to the
delegates when they dispersed.[1] Enough evidence is
extant to show that the internal organisation of the confederacy was at least as loose and defective as that of
the Hanseatic League. The jealousy of confederates rarely
permitted the ascendancy of particular members ; no canton or city enjoyed a position analogous to that of Lübeck.
Everything depended on tradition, free co-operation and
goodwill.

The survival of the Confederation proves that the state
is more important than its machinery of government. In
spite of its defective constitutional structure, the " Grand
League of Upper Germany " developed from a loose tangle
of alliances into a federal unity. The forces making for
cohesion were stronger than the forces of disintegration.
The prolonged danger from the Habsburgs made union
for defence an inveterate habit, favoured in its growth
by the traditions of communities divided by geography
and drawn together by necessity. Not only the Confederation itself, but each of its members, showed their
trust in the federal principle by entering upon a whole
series of alliances and pacts with their neighbours. Each
internal crisis showed that the habit of common action,
share in common dangers and pride in common achieve-
ments were interlaced strands in a cable stronger and
more cohesive than a written constitution or well-balanced
executive machinery. The natural hostility between rural
and urban communities was overcome by a recognition of
their equally natural inter-dependence. The Confederation
secured for its members economic freedom, control over
their hinterlands and military defence. By covenant and
sacrifice, the cities and cantons of the Alps solved the
problem of survival without surrender of autonomy ;
by a series of direct and wilful acts of sovereignty they

---

[1] These records are known as *Abschiede*, (cf. Hansa *Rezesse*). They
have been imperfectly preserved.

subjected themselves to a common power in matters which concerned all members collectively ; they accepted the democratic principle as the basis of their federal constitution and combined town and country in an organic whole.

BIBLIOGRAPHY

The historical literature on the cities of Italy and the Empire in the later Middle Ages is so vast that I have not attempted to do more than to indicate the chief sources used in writing my essay. An excellent general introduction to the bibliography of Italian cities will be found in *Revue Historique*, Tome CXX, Sept.–Oct. 1915 (" Histoire d'Italie (Moyen Age)," by René Poupardin), and in *The Cambridge Historical Journal*, Vol. I, No. I, 1923 (" Recent Work in Italian Medieval History," by C. W. Previté-Orton). For German cities a useful guide will be found in *Historiographie und Quellen der deutschen Geschichte bis* 1500, compiled by M. Sansen and L. Schmitz-Kallenberg (Leipzig and Berlin, 1914).

ORIGINAL SOURCES (GENERAL)

ALTMANN (W.) and BERNHEIM (E.) : *Ausgewählte Urkunden zur Erläuterung der Verfassungsgeschichte Deutschlands im Mittelalter*. Berlin, 1920.

BOEHMER (J.) ; *Fontes Rerum Germanicarum*. Four volumes. Stuttgart, 1843–68.

Chroniken (Die) der deutschen Städte v. 14 *bis in's* 16 *Jahrhundert*, 1862–1917.

MURATORI (J.) : *Rerum Italicarum Scriptores*. New edition from 1900. Città di Castello.

THATCHER (O. J.) and McNEAL (E. H.) ; *A Source Book for Medieval History*. New York, 1905.

VILLANI (G. M. and F.) : *Croniche*. Trieste, 1857.

WEIZSACHER (J.) : *Deutsche Reichtagsakten*. München, 1867–77.

MODERN WORKS (GENERAL)

BELOW (G. V.) : *Probleme der Wirtschaftsgeschichte*. Tübingen, 1920.

Boissonade (P.) : *Le Travail dans l'Europe chrétienne au Moyen Age.* Paris, 1921.

Grupp (G.) : *Kulturgeschichte des Mittelalters.* Volumes IV and V. Paderborn, 1914 and 1922.

Heyd (W.) : *Histoire du Commerce du Levant.* New edition. Leipzig, 1923.

Hofmann (A. v.) : *Das Land Italien und seine Geschichte.* Stuttgart and Berlin, 1921. [Historical Geography.]

Käser (K.) : *Das späte Mittelalter.* Gotha, 1921.

Kretschmer (K.) : *Historische Geographie von Mitteleuropa.* München and Berlin, 1904.

Kotzschke (R.) : *Allgemeine Wirtschaftsgeschichte des Mittelalters.* Jena, 1924.

Luchaire (J.) : *Les Démocraties italiennes.* Paris, 1915.

Pirenne (H.) : *Belgian Democracy : its early History.* Translated by J. V. Saunders. Manchester, 1915.

—— *Medieval Cities, their Origin and the Revival of Trade.*[1] Translated by F. D. Halsey. Princeton, 1925.

Yver (G.) : *Le Commerce et les Marchands dans l'Italie méridionale au xiiie et au xive Siècle.* Paris, 1903.

ITALIAN CITIES

Armstrong (E.) : *Lorenzo de' Medici.* New York and London, 1897.

Brown (H. F.) : *Venice : An Historical Sketch of the Republic.* London, 1895.

Caggese (R.) : *Firenze dalla Decadenza di Roma al Risorgimento d'Italia.* Vols. I and II. Firenze, 1912.

Davidsohn (R.) : *Geschichte von Florenz.* Four volumes. Berlin, 1896–1925.

Hertter (F.) : *Die Podestàliteratur Italiens im 12ten und 13ten Jahrhundert.* Leipzig and Berlin, 1910.

Kretschmayr (H.) : *Geschichte von Venedig.* Two volumes. Gotha, 1905 and 1920.

Douglas (L.) : *History of Siena.* London, 1902.

Lungo (I. del) : *I Bianci e i Neri.* Second edition. Milan, 1921.

Renard (G.) : *Histoire du Travail à Florence.* Two volumes. Paris, 1913–14. [Valuable for the guilds.]

Rodocanachi (E.) : *Les Institutions communales de Rome sous la Papauté.* Paris, 1901.

[1] Unfortunately I did not see this book until my essay was written.

RODOCANACHI (E.) : *Cola di Rienzo. Histoire de Rome de* 1342 *à* 1354. Paris, 1884.

RODOLICO (N.) : *La Democrazia Fiorentina nel suo Tramonto,* (1378–82). Bologna, 1905.

SALVEMINI (G.) : *Magnati e Popolani in Firenze dal* 1280 *al* 1295. Firenze, 1899.

SCHNEIDER (F.) : *Die Entstehung von Burg und Landgemeinde in Italien.* Berlin, 1924.

VILLARI (P.) : *Life and Times of Girolamo Savonarola.* Translated by L. Villari. London, 1888.

—— *Life and Times of Niccolo Machiavelli.* Translated by L. Villari. London, n.d.

—— *The Two First Centuries of Florentine History.* Translated by L. Villari. London, 1905.

TYRANNY IN ITALY

BARTOLUS OF SASSOFERATO : *Opera,* Vol. X. Bâle, 1588–9.

CESSI (R.) : *Il Malgoverno di Francesco il Vecchio, Signore di Padova.* Venezia, 1907.

PICOTTI (G. B.) : *I Caminesi e la lora signoria in Treviso.* Livorno, 1905. [Contains a valuable appendix of documents.]

SALUTATI (COLUCCIO) : *Tractatus de Tyranno.* Edited by Francesco Ercole. Berlin and Leipzig, 1914. [Contains a valuable introduction.]

SALZER (E.) : *Ueber die Anfänge der Signorie in Oberitalien.* Berlin, 1900.

URE (P. N.) : *The Origin of Tyranny.* Cambridge, 1922.

WOOLF (C. N. S.) : *Bartolus of Sassoferato.* Cambridge, 1913.

GERMAN CITIES

BELOW (G. v.) : *Entstehung der deutschen Stadtgemeinde,* 1889.

—— *Territorium und Stadt.* New edition. München and Berlin, 1923.

HEIL (B.) : *Die deutschen Städte und Bürger in Mittelalter.* Leipzig and Berlin, 1921.

—— *Die deutsche Stadt im Mittelalter.* Leipzig and Berlin. [Contains documents.]

HEGEL (K.) : *Städte und Gilden der germanischen Vöker im Mittelalter.* Two volumes, 1891.

KELLER (S.) : *Der Adelsstand des suddeutschen Patriziates.* Festschrift Otto Gierke. Weimar, 1911.

KOTZSCHKE (R.) : *Quellen zur Geschichte der Ostdeutschen Kolonisation im* 12 *bis* 14 *Jahrhundert.* Leipzig and Berlin, 1912.

—— *Grundzüge der deutschen Wirtschaftsgeschichte bis zum* 17 *Jahrhundert.* Leipzig and Berlin, 1921.

MEISTER (A.) : *Deutsche Verfassungsgeschichte von den Anfängen bis im* 15 *Jahrhundert.* Leipzig and Berlin, 1922.

SANDER (P.) : *Geschichte des deutschen Städtewesens.* Bonn and Leipzig, 1922.

SCHMOLLER (G.) : *Die Bevölkerungsbewegung der deutschen Städte von ihrem Ursprung bis im* 19 *Jahrhundert.* Festschrift Otto Gierke. Weimar, 1911.

SEELIGER (H.) : *Der Bund der Sechstädte in der Oberlausitz während der Zeit von* 1346–1437. Görlitz, 1896.

SCHWALM (J.) : *Die Landfrieden in Deutschland unter Ludwig dem Baiern.* Göttingen, 1889.

THE HANSEATIC LEAGUE.

DAENELL (E.) : *Die Blütezeit der deutschen Hanse.* Two volumes. Berlin, 1905 and 1906.

Hanserecesse. Die Recesse und andere Akten der Hansetage. Four volumes. Leipzig, 1870–6.

Hansische Geschichtsblätter, herausgegeben vom Verein für Hansische Geschichte. München und Leipzig, 1894–1917. Note especially the articles by Walther Stein, 1911–15.

LINDNER (T.) : *Die deutsche Hanse.* Leipzig, 1911.

SCHÄFER (D.) : *Die deutsche Hanse.* Bielefeld and Leipzig, 1914.

SCHNEIDER (F.) : *Die Hansa.* Leipzig and Berlin. [Documents.]

INDEX OF PERSONS AND PLACES

A

Aachen, 15
Aar, R., 193, 194, 195, 198
Abdera, 36
Accursius, 23
Adige, R., 12
Adolf of Nassau, 196
Adolf of Holstein, 15, 16
Adriatic Sea, 12
Æneas Silvius, 92
Ægeri, Lake, 197
Africa, 19, 22, 23, 26, 189
Alberigo of Barbiano, 158
Albert, Emperor, 171
Albizzi family, 74
Alessandria, 119, 125-6, 152
Alexander of Hales, 23
Alps, 2, 3, 7, 12, 13, 19, 37, 47,
    60, 110, 150, 151, 158, 160,
    163, 167-9, 177, 193, 206
Ambrose, Saint, 121, 122
America, 189
Amsterdam, 183, 188
Ancona, 159
Anjou, House of, 43, 125
Anjou, Charles of, 118-19
Antonio de Acquilo, 139
Antwerp, 35
Appennines, 82, 107, 135
Appenzell, 204
Aquinas, St. Thomas, 23, 105,
    142
Aragon, 1, 10, 43, 69, 106
Archipelago, 21
Arezzo, 74, 81, 82
Argos, 36

Aristotle, 101, 102, 103, 109, 142
Arnolfo di Cambio, 34
Arqua, 116
Asia, 18, 19, 21, 22, 26
Athens, 36, 166
Athens, Duke of, 73, 125
Atlantic Ocean, 189
Augsburg, 20, 35, 175
Augustine, St., 104
Austria, 201
Austria, Frederick of, 196
Austria, Leopold of, 176, 177,
    198

B

Baden, 198
Bâle, 11, 20, 35, 36, 47, 174, 176,
    177, 194, 199, 204
Baltic Sea, 12, 14-18, 21, 22, 33,
    36, 151, 152, 173, 178-80, 182,
    183, 187, 188, 190
Barbiano, Alberigo of, 158
Barcelona, 21, 23, 35
Bartolus of Sassoferrato, 110-12,
    131, 137-42
Bavaria, 12, 175, 176
Bavaria, Lewis of, 89, 90, 171,
    196
Bedford, 36
Belgrade, 12
Benevento, 82
Benevenuto de Castegnedo, 130
Benjamin of Tudela, 61
Bergen, 17, 20
Berlin, 164, 191
Bernadino of Siena, 135

213

Berne, 15, 176, 194, 195, 198, 203
Bernese Oberland, 194, 197
Berthoud, 15
Bienne, 205
Birmingham, 36
Black Forest, 193, 194
Black Sea, 19, 20, 21
Block, Dr. Willibald, 162
Boccaccio, 136
Bohemia, 33, 175, 177
Bohemia, Ottocar of, 17
Bologna, 29, 35, 36, 61, 66, 107, 108, 115, 119, 152
Bonn, 12
Boso di Doaria, 118
Bosphorus, 21
Brabant, 24, 30, 92
Braccio di Montone, 158, 159
Brandenburg, 186, 191
Braunsberg, 17, 18
Breisgau, 14
Bremen, 13, 27, 179, 187, 190
Brenner Pass, 19, 20
Brenta, R., 12
Brescia, 119, 152
Breslau, 186, 187, 190
Bretigny, Treaty of, 160
Bridge, J. S. C., 164
Brieg, 183
Bristol, 35
Bruges, 20, 24, 29, 35, 37, 179
Brünig Pass, 197
Brunswick, 14, 52, 92, 93, 94, 187
Brussels, 87
Brutus, 139, 141
Bryce, 149, 168
Bulgaria, 20
Burckhardt, 106
Burgundy, 7, 14, 168, 193, 197, 199
Burgundy, Duke of, 71
Burke, 165

C

Cæsar, 141
Cambio, Arnolfo di, 34
Cambrai, 45
Cambridge, 36
Caminesi, 126, 128–31, 136

Campagni, 63, 66
Capponi, 77
Cardiff, 36
Carlyle, Thomas, 2
Carmagnola, 159
Carrara, 120
Carrara, Francesco, 131
Carrara, Jacopo, 126
Carraresi, 132, 133, 136, 139
Cassino, 139, 141
Castelli, 129
Castile, 1, 10
Castruccio Castracani, 146
Catalonia, 19, 38
Cesare Borgia, 146
Ceseno, 135
Cessi, Roberto, 132
Champagne, 24, 179
Charlemagne, 81
Charles IV, Emperor, 24, 83, 92, 97, 175
Charles V, Emperor, 59
Charles I of Anjou, 118–19
Charles the Bold, 203
Charles VIII of France, 163, 165
Chester, 36
Chiana valley, 82
Chios, 21
Cicero, 101
Ciompi, Rising of 73–80, 96
Clement VII, 158, 177
Cleve, 15
Colleone, 159
Cologne, 12, 25, 27, 28, 33, 35, 36, 37, 47, 48, 87, 93–7, 174, 179, 183, 187, 190, 191
Cologne, Archbishop of, 24, 48
Como, 115
Conradin, 119
Constance, 11, 20, 90, 97, 152, 176, 177
Constantine, 155
Constantinople, 172
Copenhagen, 183
Cornelius Nepos, 138
Corsica, 21
Corso Donati, 63
Cracow, 186, 187, 190
Crecy, 160

Cremona, 47, 118, 126, 152
Cyprus, 23, 38

D

Dante, 34, 62, 106, 135, 139, 142
Danube, R., 10, 12, 20
Danzig, 18, 182, 185, 187
Dardanelles, 21
Davidsohn, 106
Denmark, 16, 168, 182, 183, 187
Diablerets, 194
Dinant, 29, 186
Döffingen, 177
Doge of Venice, 37–8, 54–6
Dorpat, 18
Dortmund, 6, 13, 15, 25, 89, 90, 97, 187, 191

E

Edward III, of England, 24, 73
Eger, Treaty of, 178
Egypt, 19
Elbe, R., 15, 89, 187, 190
Elbing, 17, 18, 183
Elborg, 183
Emperors, see Empire
Empire, Holy Roman, 2, 15, 18, 19, 43, 46, 49, 50, 104, 110, 111, 134, 137, 140, 142, 151–6, 168, 169–72, 173, 174, 179, 193, 195, 196, 200
Empoli, 81
England, 1, 8, 10, 16, 22, 31, 35, 57, 60, 65, 69, 79, 82, 99, 150, 152, 178, 180, 181, 182, 188
Ephesus, 36
Ercole, Professor F., 128
Erzgebirge, 29
Este family, 107, 116, 117, 118, 120, 125, 127, 134
Esthonia, 18
Euganean Hills, 116
Ezzelino di Romano, 123

F

Farinata degli Uberti, 62
Feldkirck, 176
Ferrara, 107, 116, 117, 118, 133, 135, 152

Ferrari, 113
Fichelgebirge, 29
Fiesole, 81
Flanders, 16, 22, 24, 29, 30, 38, 44, 47, 70, 71, 173, 180, 181
Florence, 4, 6, 21, 22–5, 26, 28–32, 34–8, 46, 53, 62, 63, 66–8, 72–86, 96, 106, 107, 109, 110, 112, 115, 118, 120, 125, 136, 139, 143–5, 153, 156, 159, 164, 165
France, 1, 10, 19, 24, 31, 61, 69, 82, 157, 161, 163, 168
Francis, St., 63
Franconian Emperors, 13
Frankfort, 35, 36, 90
Franks, 11
Frederick Barbarossa, 16, 152, 169
Frederick II, Emperor, 16, 43, 52, 62, 91, 110, 153, 154, 169, 170, 171, 173, 196
Frederick III, Emperor, 134
Frederick II of Brandenburg, 191
Frederick the Great, 100
Freeman, 148, 149
Freiburg, 14
Friburg, 15, 203, 204
Frisches Haff, 17
Frisia, 16, 173
Friuli, 131

G

Gambacorti, 108
Gattamelata, 159
Genoa, 21, 22, 35, 37, 156, 182
Germany, passim
Ghent, 24, 29, 35, 36, 37, 71
Ghibellines, 43, 54, 63, 74, 82, 110, 111, 117, 119, 120, 129, 154, 156, 157
Giotto, 34
Giovanni Vignate, 108
Glarus, 198, 203
Glossators, 101
Gonzaga, 120, 133, 134, 136
Gorlitz, 175
Goslar, 13, 187, 191

Gotland, 179, 180, 187
Göttingen, 25
Gracchi, 103
Greece, 100, 101, 108, 151
Gregory the Great, 104
Gregory VII, 45
Griefswald, 14, 18
Grisons, 194, 205
Guelfs, 43, 44, 54, 62, 63, 74, 82, 110, 111, 117–20, 123, 125–6, 129, 154, 156, 157
Guicciardini, 145–6, 165
Guido Bonacolsi, 127

H

Habsburg, Frederick of, 171, 196
Habsburg, Leopold of, 197, 198
Habsburg, Rudolf of, 156, 195
Habsburgs, 8, 176, 177, 178, 193–200
Hainault, 44
Halberstadt, 191
Halle, 90, 92, 187, 191
Hamburg, 15, 27, 35, 36, 93, 94, 174, 179, 185, 187, 190
Hanseatic League, 7, 22, 24, 92, 93, 97, 167, 174, 178–92, 206
Hardewich, 183
Hartlepool, 36
Hartz Mountains, 26, 169
Hawkwood, Sir John, 159, 160
Heidelberg, 176
Heinrich von Lohe, 94
Helmold, 16
Henley, 36
Henry III, Emperor, 13, 91
Henry VI, Emperor, 153
Henry VII, Emperor, 123, 171, 196
Henry II, of England, 152
Henry the Lion, 14, 15, 16, 52, 179
Hildesheim, 187
Hohenburg, Count Rudolf of, 176
Hohenstaufen, 2, 43, 152, 154, 156, 169
Holland, 44, 182, 188, 189
Holstein, 18, 183, 186

Holstein, Adolf of, 15, 16
Holzschuber, 92
Hoxter, 25
Hungary, 20, 166

I

Iberian Peninsula, 150
India, 189
Inn, R., 20, 194
Innocent III, 153
Innsbruck, 19
Ireland, 150
Italy, passim
Ivan III of Russia, 189

J

Jews, 18, 22, 26, 87, 171
John of Salisbury, 104
Justinian, 106

K

Kaffa, 21
Kalmar, Union of, 187
Kamenz, 175
Kampen, 187
Kettering, 36
Kieff, 188
Kolberg, 14
Königsberg, 17, 18
Kulm, 14, 17, 18

L

Labau, 175
Lambert of Hersfeld, 47
Lamprecht, 88
Legnano, 152
Leipsic, 36
Levant, 19
Liège, 29, 30, 48, 49
Lille, 24
Limmat, R., 51
Lithuania, 188
Liverpool, 36
Livonia, 17, 18, 186, 187
Loban, 175
Lodi, 46, 108
Lombard League, 152, 173
Lombards, 11

Lombardy, 12, 13, 37, 46, 61, 107, 108, 152, 158, 161, 169
London, 17, 20, 23, 24, 35, 179
Louvain, 29
Lübeck, 14–18, 22, 27, 35–7, 51–3, 56, 86, 93, 169, 174, 179, 180–5
Luca Corsini, 144
Lucca, 61, 81, 118
Lucerne, 13, 176, 197, 198, 200, 202, 203
Lucerne, Lake of, 194
Ludecke Holland, 94
Lüneburg, 13
Lusatia, 93, 175
Luxemburg Emperors, 178

M

Machiavelli, 75, 146, 161, 162–3, 165
Magdeburg, 13, 14, 17, 27. 28, 87, 93, 187
Mainz, 89, 174, 175
Malatesta, 84
Malatesta of Rimini, 135
Manfred, tailor of Treviso, 130
Mantua, 127, 133, 136, 152
Margaret of Denmark, 187
Marienwerden, 17
Marseilles, 21
Marsilius of Padua, 105, 140
Maximilian, Emperor, 172, 199
Mecklenburg, 18, 183, 186
Medici, 4, 6, 31, 75, 77, 78, 81, 107–9 139, 143–4
Mediterranean Sea, 19, 21, 26, 189
Meissen, 175
Meuse, R., 12, 46
Mezzabarba, Bishop of Florence, 46
Michele Lando, 77–9
Milan, 20, 29, 35–8, 46, 121–3, 133, 134, 138, 152, 156, 158, 159
Miletus, 36
Mocenigo, Doge of Venice, 37–8
Modena, 29, 135

Moldavia, 20
Mont Blanc, 194
Montepulciano, 82
Montferrat, William of, 125
Montford, 176
Montjoie, 158
Montorius de Villanova, 129
Montpellier, 23
Monreale, 159
Morgarten, 160, 197–8
Moselle, R., 174
Moslems, 19
Mulhouse, 205
Munich, 14, 15
Munster, 13, 89, 187
Munster, Bishop of, 47

N

Näfels, 198, 199
Naples, 21, 23, 43, 73, 134, 156, 158, 159
Napoleon, 100
Narva, 186
Nassau, Adolf of, 196
Neckar, R., 176
Netherlands, passim
Neuburg, 176
Neuchâtel, county of, 205
Neuchâtel, Lake of, 194, 198
Nicholas of Flüe, 203
Nîmes, 23
Normandy, 24
Normans, 43
North Sea, 12, 15, 24, 33, 36, 173, 178, 183, 188, 190
Norway, 16, 180, 182, 187
Novgorod, 17, 21, 180, 188, 189, 190
Nuremburg, 6–20, 35, 36, 37, 91, 92, 96, 97, 177

O

Occam, 142
Oder, R., 15
Oman, Sir Charles, 157, 158, 162, 199
Osnabrück, 89
Otto I, Emperor, 46

Otto III, Emperor, 89
Otto of Strassburg, 197
Ottocar of Bohemia, 17
Oxford, 36

P

Padua, 35, 36, 119, 126, 128, 131, 138, 139, 152
Palermo, 35
Palestine, 19
Pandolfo Petrucci, 85
Papacy, 1, 2, 6, 7, 23, 43, 46, 49, 50, 85, 104, 107, 110, 134, 135, 151, 153, 155, 156
Papal States, 43, 157, 159
Paris, 21, 23, 35, 164
Parma, 120, 125
Paul, St., 104, 112
Pavia, 61
Pennine Alps, 194
Pericles, 38
Pernau, 17, 18
Perugia, 66, 67, 111, 112, 120, 159
Petrarch, 136
Petrus de Arpo, 129-30
Piacenza, 120
Picotti, G. B., 128
Pirenne, 24, 49, 51, 69, 71
Pisa, 21, 37, 46, 61, 74, 81, 108, 110, 156, 164-5
Pistoia, 81, 118, 104
Pius II, 92
Plato, 50, 101-3
Plutarch, 138
Plymouth, 36
Po, R., 20, 117
Poland, 17, 168, 172, 175, 178, 180, 186, 188, 190
Polenta, 116
Pomerania, 18, 187
Pomerellen, 182
Popes, see Papacy
Portuguese, 189
Prato, 61, 118
Provence, 19, 61
Prussia, 16, 17, 22, 182, 184, 186, 187, 188, 190

R

Ratisbon, 12
Ravenna, 116
Regensburg, 11, 20, 171
Reggio, 115, 127, 135
Reigate, 36
Reuss, R., 193, 194, 195
Reval, 18, 179
Rhine, R., 7, 10, 12, 13, 20, 24, 29, 36, 45, 47, 174, 176-8, 190, 194, 195, 198
Rhone, R., 12, 20, 194
Rialto, Venice, 12
Ricci, 75
Rienzo, 135-6, 154-6
Riga, 18, 180, 187
Rimini, 135
Ripon, 36
Robert of Naples, 125
Robert the Wise, 73
Rodolico, Professor, 32, 74
Rolandinus of Treviso, 130
Romagna, 158
Romania, 38
Rome, 54, 81, 82, 118, 136, 154-6
Romeo Pepoli, 108
Roncaglia, Diet of, 152
Roosebeeke, 71
Rostock, 14, 18, 93, 97, 179-83, 187
Rotenburg, 177
Rottweil, 205
Rudolph Brun, 98, 197
Rupert, Emperor, 90, 97
Russia, 16, 17, 22, 172, 178, 179, 185, 189, 190

S

Saint-Gall, 205
Saint Gotthard Pass, 13, 20, 194, 195, 198, 201
Salinguerra, 117
Salisbury, 36
Salonica, 69
Salutati, Coluccio, 128, 137, 139-42
Salzer, Dr., 121
Salzwedel, 191

Samos, 36
San Gimignano, 61
San Giorgio d'Orsi, 118
Savonarola, 86, 143, 145
Saxony, 16, 33, 186, 187
Scala family, 120, 124
Scandinavia, 1, 172, 173, 178, 182, 190
Scania, 182–3, 188
Schaffhausen, 90, 198, 204
Scheldt, R., 12
Schleswig, 183
Schwyz, 194–8, 200, 202, 203
Scotland, 92, 150, 182
Sebald, St., 91
Seine, R., 20
Sempach, 177, 198–201, 204
Seneca, 103
Sforza, Attendola, 158, 159
Shrewsbury, 36
Sicily, 19, 22, 38, 43
Siena, 46, 63, 66–8, 72–4, 81–6, 96, 109, 135
Sigismund, Emperor, 91, 93, 97, 134
Sigmund Miersterlin, 91, 92
Silesia, 175, 186
Soest, 13, 14, 16, 89, 187
Soleure, 176, 203, 204
Sonzino, 118
Spain, 19, 31, 157, 189
Sparta, 36, 166
Speyer, 174
Spires, 47
Splügen Pass, 20
Stanz, 200, 201, 204
Stecknitz Canal, 15
Stein, Dr. Walther, 180, 181, 186
Stendal, 27, 191
Stettin, 18
Stockholm, 180
Stralsund, 18, 182, 183, 185, 187, 190
Strassburg, 12, 35, 36, 37, 47, 171, 174, 175, 177
Stratford-on-Avon, 36
Suabia, 175, 176, 177, 193
Suabian League, 7, 175, 177, 178, 202

Sweden, 182–3, 187
Switzerland, 3, 7, 8, 151, 177, 193–207
Symonds, 108
Syracuse, 36

T

Taddeo de Pepoli, 107
Tagliacozzo, 82
Teutonic Order, 2, 16, 17, 59
Thebes, 36
Theiss, R., 12
Theodoric, 146
Thorn, 17, 18, 183, 188
Thuringia, 177
Ticino, R., 194
Torriano, 122, 123
Toulouse, 61
Trasimene, Lake, 81
Trave, R., 15
Traversari, 116
Treviso, 126–7, 128–31, 138, 152
Tudor Kings of England, 65
Tuscan League, 153
Tuscany, 30, 61, 72, 74, 81, 82, 85, 107, 109, 118, 136, 153, 157, 169
Tyrol, 33, 194

U

Uberto Palavacini, 125
Ulm, 20, 36, 175, 177
Umbria, 153
United States of America, 149
Unterwalden, 194–7, 200, 202
Urban VI, 158
Ure, P. N., 107, 108
Uri, 194–5, 196, 200, 202

V

Valais, 205
Val d'Elsa, 81
Van Artevelde, 6
Venetia, 161
Venice, 4, 6, 12, 19, 20, 21, 22, 26, 29, 35–8, 51, 53–9, 61, 72, 92, 98, 107, 109, 110, 134, 144, 148, 152, 155, 156, 159, 164, 172, 182

Verona, 29, 96, 61, 121, 123-4, 133, 152, 156
Via Æmilia, 82
Via Passia, 81
Vicenza, 119, 152
Vienna, 15, 20
Villani, 31, 34, 113, 136
Villari, 164
Visconti, 46, 85, 120, 122-3, 125, 134, 136, 139
Visconti, Gian Galeazzo, 100, 131
Visconti, Ottone, 122
Vistula, R., 15, 17, 188, 190
Vosges Mountains, 177

W

Wäggi Tal, 202
Waldemar III of Denmark, 182-3, 187
Wales, 150
Ware, 36
Warsaw, 17
Wenceslas, Emperor, 134, 175, 176, 177, 178, 202

Weser, R., 13, 89, 187, 190
Wisby, 179, 180, 182, 186
Wismar, 14, 15, 93, 179, 182, 183, 185
Wittelsbach, House of, 91, 196
Worcester, 36
Worms, 47, 48, 174, 178
Wurtemburg, Count of, 176, 177

Y

Ypres, 29, 35, 36, 70

Z

Zähringen, Berthold of, 15
Zähringen, Conrad of, 14
Zähringen, family, 14, 15
Zeeland, 188, 189
Zittau, 175
Zug, 176, 197, 198, 200, 202, 203
Zurich, 11, 29, 35, 51, 56, 98, 176, 194, 197, 198, 200
Zurich, Lake of, 198